Two Hearts Forever Strong

CROSSROADS

CROSSROADS

Tommy's Book of Poetry III

TOMMY RHYS ANDREWS

ISBN:	Softcover	978-1-9845-9208-8
	eBook	978-1-9845-9207-1

Print information available on the last page.

Rev. date: 10/09/2019

To order additional copies of this book, contact:
Xlibris
800-056-3182
www.Xlibrispublishing.co.uk
Orders@Xlibrispublishing.co.uk
804047

Chapter List

Part I – The Alternate Route

Part II – The Journey Continues

Other Books by Author

Foothpath- Published 10/21/2010
Stepping Stones- Published 7/10/2017

Part I

Chapter 1

A Footpath through the Wilderness.

Introduction

My name is Tommy, some know me as Matt.
I have written for the last decade
Through good and bad. Through this and that.
Many types of rhymes, through all different times
For all different reasons, for every single crime.
These rhymes will tell a story
Of a mind which can be strange.
All different genres, there's a wide range.
Now I'm ready to let people
Know the truth about me.
The truth of these thoughts
I need to break free.
Take your time to acknowledge
What I have to say.
And one more thing…
…HAVE A NICE DAY!!

Visually Correct

Camera Cat,
Stop and stare,
Share the secrets
That you share.
The things that you think
Each time that you blink
Will baffle your brain
With each sip that you drink.
You look over and wink,
The lies start to sink
The differences are opposites
With no sign of interlink.

What lingers your mind?
What truth will you find?
As you sit down and don't mind
How angry or kind
Your mind can get left behind.

Now how do you feel?
You're learning what's real
You're getting a deal
With your happy meal.

These brainwaves will visualize,
You're learning to realise
As your thought plan will race,
You see the look on your face.
You see in your head
Those images you dread,
Your brain cells will shred
Those things that you've said
To yourself whilst alone
That night in your home
With your telephone.

Are you reading these lines?
What truth will you find?

You see what I got,
You can like it or not.
Is that a grammar dissect?
Well, it's visually correct.

Do you feel the same?
What is this game?
Allow me to explain
As you look out to the rain
And up to the moon
Whilst hearing that tune
Twelve hours after noon.

I hear you there,
Acting like you don't care,
What truth does this share?
Do you think that life's fair?
You sit and you stare
In darkness, I swear.
As you pull on your hair,
With less than Tony Blair
Watching those videos of Bare
In those clothes that you wear,
With your shoes in a pair.

As you look through your eyes
And to your surprise,
There aren't any lies,
Don't run down that road
It may not be wise.

I've been waiting
For the opportunity
To create a revelation
In your community,
To establish my name
Inside this galaxy,
It would change people's thoughts
About true reality.

Now, put down the paint and grout,
Learn what I'm all about.
Learn what makes people cry.
What makes people wonder why?
What makes people shout?

I'm starting a revelation,
A path for people to follow,
A path that can help you
Change the thoughts of tomorrow.
A path to make you think
About what put you here on Earth,
A path to determine
Your life to death from birth.

Take the stand that you need,
For your truth, you'll sweat and bleed.
You will come to a realisation,
You will stand before your nation,
You will take control, indeed.

Because we're all here
To keep walking each footpath.
So, cleanse your emotions.
Wash them away in a holy bath.
Walk forward, make your move
To the rhythm, you'll be a dancer,
If you keep exploring the question,
You will soon find the answer.

Inspector Goole

There's a knock
On the door
Gerald drinks port
But Eric has more.

The inspector begins
To walk inside.
Birling family,
There's nowhere to hide.

He'll question you all
One at a time
He'll make you confess
To committing a crime.

Eva killed herself
Because of you,
You better believe him
Because this is all true.

Authur kicked her
Out of her job,
That's why she had reasons
To sit and to sob.

Sheila had Eva sacked
Because she felt she should,
She thought she was laughed at
By Eva in Milwards.

Gerald had an affair
With Eva, I mean Daisy.
It doesn't matter her name,
The whole thing is crazy.

Daisy became pregnant
With Eric's child.
My gosh, this family
Is truly wild.

Because of Sybyl
And her frustrations,
Eva was refused help at
The Brumley's Women's Charity Organisation.

The inspector got each
Member to confess,
You have got to admit
That this whole thing's a mess.

He questioned them all
One by one,
There was no stopping the chaos
Once it begun.

He made each person
Feel like a fool,
Who was this man?
He's Inspector Goole!

Super Sis (Part I)

Where can I start?
What can I say?
Stephanie, I wish that you
Were with me today.

I miss seeing your face,
Dear lord, this is true,
I really miss all
There is about you.

Now you are fine,
No longer in pain.
The thought of you suffering
Would drive me insane.

You no longer suffer,
I worry no more,
You no longer hurt,
You're no longer sore.

I thank the lord now
That you're well and fine,
Whose sister are you?
Stephanie, you're mine!

Hero

What is a hero?
A man with a mask?
A man who follows rules
To accomplish his task?

What is a hero?
A man who risks his life?
A man who don't need
The use of a knife?

What is a hero?
A man who will do
Whatever it takes
To be there to help you.

A man with a plan,
A countdown to zero?
You need not a cape
To be a true hero.

Will You?

When I'm in trouble,
Will you be there?
When things get hard,
Will you show that you care?

When I can't cope with life,
Will you help me get better?
When we're miles away,
Will you write me a letter?

When I'm old and disabled,
Will you help me to drive?
When I'm stuck in the gutter,
Will you help me survive?

When I'm going through problems,
Will you help me?
Because I'll always help you,
I hope that you see.

When you need my help,
I'll help you get through.
You're the best friend I've got,
When I need your help, will you?

True Art

With anger and rage
As I clench my fist,
Not knowing which way
This fate will twist.

Unable to explain
How she makes me feel,
Making me suffer,
This pain is unreal.

The attitude she shows,
The signs of a witch.
All I can say
Is that she gave me an itch.

Striking shots of fear
Down each of our spines,
Sharing her lack of compassion
For each of who whines.

Making us unhappy,
Enraging our emotions,
I could picture this witch
Mixing her potions.

Using her voodoo dolls
To make us all suffer.
She has the art of a liar,
The art of a bluffer.

Hidden Movement

The truth is now known,
These feelings are now shown.
Your thoughts have now grown,
You can see into the unknown.

Just sit down and stare
Into the door right there.
Take this dare
And the secrets will share.

Don't move at all,
This door in front of the wall,
You will begin to fall
And take your sole role.

You'll begin to move
Deep into this groove,
You'll rise from the floor
And walk through the door.

Someone

Someone with power,
Someone who cares,
Someone who shares
Any problem there is.

Someone with a flower,
Someone who'll do
Anything for happiness
Anything for you.

Someone with an hour
To do you a favour,
Someone who'll give you
Your favourite flavour.

Someone with a shower
To wash away your feelings,
Someone with a band-aid
Whenever you're bleeding.

Someone from above,
Someone who's there,
Someone with love,
Someone who cares.

Free (Part I)

Tick Tock,
Which way will you think?
Tick tock,
You sit with your drink.

Tick tock,
You drown in your sorrow.
Tick tock,
You fear tomorrow.

Tick tock,
You're scared of what's true.
Tick tock,
You fear that voice inside you.

Tick tock,
You're feeling so hollow.
Tick tock,
Which path will you follow?

Tick tock,
Listen to me.
Tick tock,
It's time to break free.

What I Like

My name is Tommy,
I'm from Wales,
I have some stories,
I have some tales.
I don't like beer,
I don't like ales,
I don't weigh much
When I step on the scales.

I like to sing
While I'm in the bath,
I like to mess around
Just for a laugh.
I've seen a pink elephant
And an orange giraffe,
But probably because I was drunk
From drinking whiskey and stuff.

I like my friends
As you can tell,
I may be possessed
And I may have seen hell.
I like my hair,
I like to use gel,
Probably because
I don't like the smell.

When I'm old
And dying and ill,
I want to go on a journey
Over to Brazil.
I have one more thing
That I want in my will,
And that's to leave my Xbox
To my ex worker, Phil.

Test Paper

Using your paper
And using your pen,
You are doing your
Practice paper again.

You're answering questions
From one to whatever,
If you answer them all
You would feel so clever.

You're answering questions,
You reach question three,
You answer them all
With help from your PC.

If you're too tired to work,
You should stay in bed,
So do your own work,
And don't copy me instead.

Mirror

Such a piece of art
Gone to waste,
Like too much red wine
On the steak to spoil the taste.

All the smudges and scratches,
And a crack down the side,
It really must have gone
For one final last ride.

Still sitting there leaned back
Against the hard-wooden door.
The bad shiny mirror
Is now situated on the wall, not the floor.

Death

Point a gun
To my head,
Pull the trigger
And I'd be dead.
Suck it out
With a pump,
Get a band-aid
To patch the lump

In the heart
With a knife,
Any way
To end my life.
Use some magic
To sew it closed.
Then wash it over
With a fire hose.

In the eye
With a pen,
Over and over,
Again, and again.
Stop the time,
Click rewind.
You'll watch the eye
Become not blind.

Put bricks in my pockets
And jump in a river.
Freeze to death,
Can't help but shiver.
Pockets will rip,
Bricks will fall out.
We wash onto the shore
Our inner fire starts to shout

Drink fifty pints of Pepsi,
I'm drowned but I'm dry.
Nobody will miss me,
Nobody would cry.
Spew out the Pepsi,
I inhale fresh air.
A sign from beyond
Which shows that life's there.

Jump in a pool
Full of maggots.
Put me in the microwave
With your peas and faggots.
The pool will explode,
You again become free,
The microwave couldn't
Put enough radiation in me.

Stick a ten-inch pencil
Up my nose,
It goes through my brain,
I then chop off my toes.
Pull out the pencil,
Carefully keeping the brain within,
I grow some new toes,
Now where do I begin?

I smash a telly
With my head.
Come on now surely
I must be dead.
The telly couldn't have
Been plugged in,
Now I must place
It in the bin.

I tip some acid
Into my eyes,
They dissolve
To my surprise.
Lucky for me,
The nerves remain,
My sight returns
Thanks to signals in the brain.

I've died more than once,
I have blood on my shirt.
I rip out my tonsils,
Which kind of hurt.
Lucky for me
It cured my tonsillitis,
It's almost as if
Death truly wants to fight us

I hang myself
With a rope I scoped.
"I'm dead by now" ...
So, I hoped.
Before I see,
The rope starts to break.
There was a fault in the design,
This was no mistake.

I slit my wrist
Just in case.
Just hit me with a shovel
Across the face.
I glue the wound
It then heals faster,
And I cover my head
With a rectangular plaster.
I soak myself with petrol,
I set myself on fire,
I hang myself again
But I raise the rope higher.
As luck would have it,
The fire causes the rope to snap
I fall below the podium
I then land softly
In a tub full of sodium

I slash my throat
With a blade,
You see my life
Begin to fade.
A paramedic arrives
Around my neck, he places a scarf,
This helps me survive,
The next day, I had a laugh.

I pull out my eyeballs
With a cocktail stick,
Do not try this at home,
It is not a magic trick.
But what would you know?
I put on some cream,
Before waking up in the morning
And realising it was a dream.

Frequency

I am so desperate,
I am so keen
To just go home
And look at my TV screen.

I could watch the news
Or even "The Bill",
I remind myself that my remote
Is placed upon the window sill.

I turn on the telly,
It begins then.
I have seen this episode
Again, and again.

I've been so keen
To watch this TV.
There is nothing on
That appeals to me.

There's nothing on E4,
BBC or ITV,
I could watch some cartoons
Like Dexter or Ed, Edd and Eddy.

After a thorough examination
Of my propaganda choice,
I turn on my radio
And I lift my singing voice.

The Answers to the Questions

The answers to the questions
That we all share,
These questions, we all wonder.
Are the answers possibly there?

The questions that lingers
At the back of our mind,
The question that's shared
Through all of mankind.

The answers that explains
Every question that there is.
The questions that makes our brains
Sizzle and fizz.

The questions that make us wonder
Why we want to give,
The questions that we wonder
Each day as we live.

Who knows the answers
To the questions that we think?
The questions that we wonder,
Like what makes us blink and makes us wink?

The answers are out there
For everyone that wants to know,
The answers to the questions
That we all wonder so.

All True

Take this time to listen
To what I have to say,
On this fine seeming day,
This poem isn't a made-up play.

I have a voice within my head
That takes over my mind,
I have a voice that's unkind
This makes me feel so blind.

I tried to run, I tried to hide,
There was nowhere that I could go,
I couldn't tell this voice no,
Only now people know.

I kept it to myself for such a long time,
My family and friends
Now know the truth with no bends,
From the beginning until the end.

There's a voice in the background,
He took over my life,
He even held a knife
And tried to self sacrifice.

He overdosed on paracetamol,
He tried to end it all,
With no hesitation, with no stall,
True enough, he made my life fall.

He took control of me
He made me see
The things that couldn't be,
I knew I wasn't free.

Escape was impossible,
He had a grip supported by wrath,
He took away the path
This made me overlook the aftermath.

They are always around me,
He was a part of my head,
He will never be dead,
Did you hear what I said?

In the mind is where it begins,
They are extremely controlling,
They're there, I feel them staring
At me in the mirror, they cannot win.

You may not believe this,
You may not think its true,
But Tommy is not lying,
This I promise you.

Gypsies

Rust on the door,
No bedroom in their caravan,
No need for council tax,
Living free like superman.

Stealing all their possessions
From places like car boot sales,
They roam the streets alone,
Sharing fairytales.

Their filthy rotten floorboards,
And half of them are gone,
The world would be a better place
If we could all just get on.

All bacteria infested,
They have cold sores on their lippies,
That's the story
Of these roaming gypsies.

Finally

In the darkness is where I was,
Feeling nothing, all because
I had no place to go and no place to think,
It was like a downward spiral inside a kitchen sink.

I pulled myself up and I found the path
That I needed to escape the wrath.
I feel human, once again,
I no longer want to self inflict pain.

Now Tommy is back and better than before.
I have escaped my emotional war.
I've picked myself up from the ground,
My newly improved life has been found.

I now no longer think about the past,
I live for the moment and make the present last.
The future always matters, I see, believe me.
I know what it feels like to be extremely happy.

Have a Nice Day

I sit here in front of the screen,
Trying to explain what I mean.
I cannot say what is in my mind,
Knowing that things to say can be hard to find.

I drift through my life as I usually do,
Not knowing what to say, I struggle to pull through.
I repeat my words, maybe five or six times,
But I don't struggle to think of a word that rhymes.

I write and I type, I talk, and I think,
I occupy my time, because I don't drink.
What else can I do? What else can I say?
Nothing except…HAVE A NICE DAY!!

Extra Fries

Here I am,
One two three.
Am I who
I'm meant to be?

I am here,
Zero, one two,
What am I
Supposed to do?

I stand up tall,
Two one half,
This life's a game of ball,
No need to laugh.

A Numeric-letter spell,
My head rings a bell,
Eight, nine, ten,
Here I go again.

Round and round,
My head will spin,
Now where could I
Even possibly begin?

Clean mind run,
Each rhyme, each time.
Not boring or fun,
Clean mind, no crime.

No sense to you,
But all to me.
I attempt to place thoughts
How they are meant to be.

I write each line
Before it's forgot,
I'm like a fast typing,
Rhyming crazy, anti-gravity robot.

I write these words explaining how I feel,
Not knowing at all if most of it is real,
My life feels like a one pound and ninety-nine pence
Extra large fries with a happy meal.

Have a Nice Night

Why do I
Just want to cry
As I sit in my bed
Wondering when I'll die.

I feel so insane; I look out to the rain,
I feel the pressure and strain,
I'm in the mood
For inflicting some pain.

I've "had my nice day!"
It's now time to pay.
I've now had enough,
What else can I say?

I look like a nerd,
Not free like a bird,
I have feelings inside
Making me feel obscured.

Ignore the feelings, ignore the emotions,
I feel like a fool,
I just want to drown
In a four-foot swimming pool.

I just want to fight,
I have a raging sight,
So, from now until then…
…Have A Nice Night!!

2010

Like a breath of heaven,
The sea-salty air,
Problems blown away,
There's no need to care.

The bittersweet coldness,
Eliminated by beach-fire.
The ice-cold sea.
A tent on the field which is higher.

A beam of sunshine,
On the frost covered grass,
With the sweet taste of Martini
As I sip from the glass.

A day of awakening,
A new start again,
A reborn life
In the year 2010.

Fast and Slow

Where shall I start?
Where shall I begin?
I sit down,
As I hold this pen.

I scribble and I jot
Word after word.
Not knowing what to say
May sound obscured.

But a meaningful subject
Makes me feel kind,
For me to write this,
I must be out of my mind.

I must clench the pen,
I must write fast
Before the thoughts in my head
Vanish to the past.

This long useless poem
That I want to write
Could probably keep me
Up all night.

Due to my forgetful memory,
This poem has reached its peak.
But remember who you are
These are the words that I speak.

Like

Like a nail in my cheek,
And not the one on my face.
Yes, a pain in my backside,
It feels like a disgrace.

Like being stuck in the rain,
Half naked with no coat.
Whilst stuck on the docks
With no roof on the boat.

Like a mirror on the wall
With a reflection looking back,
Giving that evil stare
Like I want to attack.

With no emotions to feel,
No love and no hate,
Like a tramp in the Whitehouse,
It's just not his fate.

Like stuck on a math problem,
The answer I don't know,
I don't even understand the question,
This really does blow.

Like a lyric missing
From Billy Ray Cirus,
Like having cyber
Without wearing an antivirus.

Like throwing a dart
In the opposite direction,
Like going to a shoot-out
Without wearing protection.

Like a water balloon
That explodes too soon,
Like soaking your face
In the middle of noon.

Like no reason to smile
And no reason to cry,
Like not caring for anything
And not caring why.

Like telling a joke
Without a punch-line,
Like crying your eyes out
Whilst pretending you're fine

Like throwing a tantrum
And lobbing your phone
Full force at the wall
Because you hate being alone.

Like listening to music
Without any words,
Messing up the mind
Feeling so obscured.

Like wearing shorts
With an extra-large belt,
Knowing that the feelings cannot be right,
Even though you don't know what you felt.

Like a drink of Pepsi
Which has been spiked,
Like overusing a word,
Like using the word "like".

The Real Tommy (Part I)

Sat in darkness for so long just dwelling
About my past without a smile.
I sit with the sunshine giving me brightness
There's light in my life for the first time in such a while.

Here I am, walking forward. I also see my friends.
I live my life to the fullest, from now until the end.
Nobody knows the dark secrets that I hold within,
Nobody knows, not even my next to kin.

But it's in the past,
I'm free at last,
I now run fast
Whilst having a blast.

This is my life, nobody can distract.
I have already set my goals, now that is a fact.
Here I am, now I see
Who I really am, this is the real Tommy.

I'm Back

My name is Tommy,
I'm back and I'm free,
Please welcome me back
As the king of poetry.

Where was the crime
When I gave up last time?
I gave up on writing
My poems and my rhymes.

Now I've returned and I'm placed in this game,
I'm no linger the same,
I've returned with a vengeance.
This time, you'll remember my name.

You all know me,
Matt and Tommy,
This time I'm here forever,
I don't have to force you to see.

I came back today
Because I have a lot to say.
From now until next time…
…Have a Nice Day!!

Poetry

The stress that I feel
Rushing through my head,
Each time that I write,
Nobody cares what I said.

These things that I write,
Am I wasting my time?
Does it really matter
If I write another rhyme?

The poems that I write,
It's what keeps me happy,
It helps me to structure my thoughts
And organise truth, you see?

Another poem written,
Another poem wasted.
I canst stand to think
Of the sickening things that's tasted.

Adrenaline rush of hate
Rushes quickly through my veins,
You wouldn't understand why
I self inflict pain.

Words on my arms
That I carve with a knife
Is still not as comforting
As using "word-life".

The truth is
I have problems I cannot tell,
I do positive activities
To keep my soul well from hell.

I will write these poems
Time after time
I'm not even bothered
If I've already used this rhyme.

The day I stop writing
Is still yet to happen,
Poetry's in my thoughts
It's been passed through generations.

Poetry is the sort of thing
That I like to do.
It's what I forever will be
Dedicated to.

One True Friend (Part I)

The friend I know
That's always there,
The friend I hope
Will go nowhere.

A good friend,
A special friend,
I'm here for you
Until the end.

I trust you
In every single way,
You help me to
Survive the day.

A friend I care for,
You are no fool,
My one true friend,
You are so cool.

I'll help you out
In any kind of way,
So long as you're my friend
Through every single day.

I'm always here,
I'm here until the end.
Because you really are
My one true friend.

Away

I'm sitting here
Thinking of you,
It's the kind of thing
That I like to do.

I can't get you
Out of my mind,
I can't stop thinking
That you're amazingly kind.

I'm no longer
At my place,
I miss the smile
That you show on your face.

I love your company,
Please don't hurt me,
I enjoy spending quality time,
I hope that you see.

I know that I miss you,
You're a wonderful friend,
I will always share love
From now until the end.

My Teachers

Parry looks like a carrot,
Charles acts so bold,
Gwenllian acts rather weird,
Mrs Davies's room is cold.

Mrs Owen is awesome,
Mrs Cartwright has a twitch,
I'm surprised she hasn't fallen
Down a five-foot ditch.

Humphreys is odd,
Porter is class,
I'm surprised Mrs Thompson
Hasn't fallen into the grass.

Dr Ellis collects fossils,
Don't worry; I've got their back...
Mrs Harries walks around
Always dressed in black.

Mr Rodgers who teaches sports yells
Because I won't play football.
Guess what my teachers…
…I miss you all.

Roses & Violets

Roses aren't green,
Violets aren't pink,
Here's a way of telling you
What I think.

Roses aren't yellow,
Violets aren't white
But I think of you
Every single night.

Roses aren't gold,
Violets aren't grey,
Please listen to what
I have to say.

Roses aren't silver,
Violets aren't black,
If I was to lose you,
I'd have a major setback.

But roses are red,
And violets are blue,
No girl on the earth
Makes me as happy as you.

Grandpa's Birthday

Days have gone,
Seventy-one at last
Your birthday is here,
The days have passed.

Here's a card and a poem
Just for you,
But that's not all,
You have a present too.

So, it's your birthday,
What more can I say?
Nothing except...
...Happy Birthday!!

Alone

He sits on a bus
Where people talk around,
No matter where he looks
People make a sound.

People gossip, people talk
And people have a chat.
There's a conversation for everyone
Except poor old Matt.

He sits down with a book,
His self, he'll entertain.
Why must people that's happy
Put him through this pain?

People won't share a word with him,
They won't even look,
That's why he sits alone
With his favourite book.

He sits down, on his own
He has nothing to do
All because of these people
And the things that they put him through,

On the seat, look.
Over there, you will see
That the poor boy is all alone,
He feel's that's how it'll always be.

The Wait

Why am I waiting?
It's much too much pain.
I'm just dying to get
On that fast riding train.

Why am I waiting?
I just cannot see,
Tomorrow I'll be there
By at least nine thirty.

Why am I waiting?
Am I just lazy?
Why must I wait?
I must be crazy.

I cannot stand it.
Is this my fate?
Why am I waiting?
I just cannot wait.

One True Friend (Part II)

Tears fall to the ground
Day after day,
Take this time to listen
To what I have to say.

People say that I'm sad
And say I'm insane.
You don't understand my pain
Again, and again.

What is this?
This is not a frown,
Something has happened
It has turned upside down.

Something keeps happening,
I continue to smile.
Can I be happy?
It's been such a long while.

I haven't smiled since
I cannot remember when.
I just hope my sadness
Comes to an end.

For the first time
Everyone can see,
My emotions have changed,
I'm finally happy.

For this, I thank somebody,
Do you want to know who?
The person I thanked at this time
Was Loopy Lowri Loo.

True Love

How is it that
I came to find
A beautiful girl
Who is so kind.

We share love for each other,
This I do know.
I love her so much
In ways I can't show.

My angel from above,
With whom I fell in love,
We're in each other's back pockets
Like a well fitted glove.

I enjoy each day
That I spend with this girl.
The truth is that she
Is my whole entire world.

With her beautiful face
And her soft gentle touch,
What more can I say to her?
Apart from "I love you so much".

Wishes

I wish I knew that words
To explain how I feel,
I wish I knew the difference
Between what's fake and what's real.

I wish that I could just sit back
And turn back time.
I wish I could explain how I feel
In words that could rhyme.

I wish I could change
How things turned out,
I wish I didn't have to sit here
In regret whilst I pout.

I wish my mind would forget
About things in my past,
Some happy memories still make me cry,
I wish they wouldn't care.

Who I Am

I'm not this person who you think
I may still smoke, but I no longer drink.
I have found a path which I must follow,
I must no longer drown my life in sorrow.

I no longer care
If you dislike me anymore
With this silver crucifix that I've worn once before,
There's no more pain, I no longer feel sore.

I found a path, a way to live,
And to be free at last.
No longer caring about
Things from my past.

This is just me,
Here I am again,
I still feel matt around me.
Almost like he's talking to me from within.

I hear his every word; we all have an advantage,
I'm no longer on a raging rampage.
No more pain, I just laughed,
My emotional war has been halved.

I'm Tommy, I'm Matt,
I'm whatever you want to call me.
I'm Tomato! Yes, fancy that?
Multi-people, many combined, it's now that I see.

Two is better than one,
It's about to begin,
This is a strange idea of fun,
I'm no longer on the run.

I have a plan in my head,
I no longer wish that I were dead,
There are things in my time that I have said,
Now I feel like two, like hovis best of both bread.

Because I am here,
I'm no longer on the mend.
I am already feeling fixed!
Yes, this is the end.

The Teacher

Late for lesson
Once again,
Ready for detention,
My goodness, what a shame.

I suffer my homework,
I do badly in class.
I do worse in my tests,
I never pass.

The teacher looks at me
With her evil glare,
I try not to look,
I try not to stare.

It's now too late,
She shouts at me now.
Something happened
But I cannot explain how.

I made some mistakes,
But everyone does.
But she picks on me
Out of all the others.

She picks on me,
She doesn't leave me alone.
I do not like school,
I wish I was home.

She calls in my parents
And says that I've been bad,
She shouts at me more,
It makes me so sad.

I dislike this teacher
And she doesn't like me.
She fails me on purpose,
Don't you see?

She is evil,
She'll never apologise,
Like I said, she's evil,
Just look into her eyes.

Lesson Learned (Part I)

I learned my lesson
By introducing her to him,
He's one of the ones
That made my life seem dim.

There was a time where I hated him,
I thought it was true,
But looking back now,
I pray he pulled through.

Guess what? I'm back,
Myself once again,
Next time, I won't be the one
Who's going insane.

To think of the misery,
In not knowing what to do.
The thought of the threats
That they can place into you.

They better keep their distance
That way I can keep a grip,
Because imagine what could be done
If the enemy was to slip.

We can be happy once again,
Well, at least for today.
So dark one, keep away
So that we can Have a Nice Day!!

The Real Tommy (Part II)

There I was
Sat at school,
In sixth form,
It felt rather cool.

I sat down
And I read a book
Which contained information on the lessons
Of the subjects I took.

There was welsh, media
And drama in whole,
You may think I'm daft
Or even a fool.

I had to re-sit
My maths exam twice
It contributed to the proof
Of the fact that I am nice.

I had to focus on school,
Kickboxing and work,
Whilst balancing my mind
To stop me going bezerk.

This is my new life,
I hope that you see,
So, let me show you
The real Tommy.

Good Bye

I grab a small white
Swan filter tip,
Before I continue,
I hold my Pepsi and I sip.

I pick up my green
Easy rolling papers.
I turn on my music
And listen to sky scrapers.

I place the filter in the paper
I pick up my pouch
Of Marlboro rolling tobacco
As I sit on the couch.

I manoeuvre my hands
And I roll them so thin,
I make the tobacco last longer,
I prepare to begin.

I place it to my lips
I hold my Zippo lighter,
But to win this war
I must prove I'm a fighter.

I will hold up my rollie,
I will throw it to the sky,
I don't need them anymore
Cigarette's, good bye.

Rage

Why do you make
Me feel so small?
It makes me feel like driving
My fist through a wall.

I feel like
Pulling my hair out
You know exactly what
I'm talking about.

You make me feel such
Emotional pain.
It makes me feel like
I'm going insane.

I've had enough of people
Making me feel this way,
Now leave me alone
And have a nice day!!

Back away from my bubble,
Step away from me
Because all I want to do
Is relax by a tree.

How Many

How many rhymes
Have I written so far?
How many times
Do I travel away far?

How many times
Do I try to succeed?
How many times
Have I fallen for weed?

How many times
Have I felt like I failed?
Always feel like I'm in trouble
Yet I've never been jailed.

How can I explain
All that I've been through?
What more can I say?
What more can I do?

Pylons

Electric flows
Quickly, so fast.
It powers your TV set
It makes commercial goods last.

It flows to your radio
So that you can chose
Whether you want to listen to music
Or maybe even the news.

Even though they're handy,
They have many downfalls,
A few of which are the fact that
They are dangerous and tall.

They give power to power plants
Where their systems run on an automatic lock,
You must not touch the wires
Or you'd get a nasty shock.

Pylons are dangerous,
I hope that you see.
Nobody complains though
Because they are so handy.

So that is the end of this
Bizarre poem today,
Oh yeah, one more thing...
Have A Shockingly Nice Day!!

Turkey

Get two turkeys
To have a race,
Bet on the one
With the weird face.

You wait to see
Which is the winner,
Then you cook it for
Your Christmas dinner.

You go to the shop
To buy another,
But it's still alive
And it starts chasing your mother.

Your mother can't win,
The turkey's too fat,
And it starts chasing her
With a baseball bat.

The turkey caught her,
The clucking thing is insane,
It puts the family
Through an eggstreme amount of pain.

Get that turkey,
Did you hear what I said?
There's no need to bother,
Because it dropped dead.

Poem of Neutrality (Part I)

Dear lord,
What can I say?
Take this time to listen
To what I have to say.

To talk about someone
And how he betrayed me,
I decided to mess around
With a special person, you see?

I wanted him
To drive off far in a car,
As I slept in my bed
And drifted away far.

For having these thoughts,
I must have been sad,
There were things going wrong
Which was driving me mad.

Thinking of that man,
As well as other stuff,
At the time, I felt like
I truly had enough.

I had some issues,
I hope that you see that it's true,
Guess what people?
Positivity will pull you through.

The Chair (Part I)

I want to write a poem,
But I don't know what to say.
I want to write something
Due to the boredom that I feel today.
I hope I write something
That does not get in the way
Of the day to day activities
And where I rest as I lay.

Should I write about life?
Maybe death or love?
Or maybe write about the angels
Which love to fly above.
I could write about the birds
And mention a white dove
Or of how I keep my hands together
As I pray, like a human glove.

Should I write about my family?
Or maybe I should study the systems of school…
Whatever is decided,
It's doesn't matter if it's cool.
I could attempt to explain cryptology
But I may sound a fool,
Instead I'll mention geometry
Like a bird's eye view whilst playing pool.

What should I write about?
I really don't know.
Maybe I should write of
The expressions that I show.
Like when I'm happy
My smile will grow
Because the power of positivity
Is something I like to show.

I know what I'll write about
I knew that it would be there,
I didn't know before,
I had no reason to care.
But I look over in the corner,
I glare and I stare
At the item which I write about,
It's my Bluetooth armchair.

Periods of Transition

The things that I think
When I don't sleep at night,
The things that fills
My eyes with fright,

I get the thought
Of when she parted from me,
If only that reality
Was meant to be.

I thought that we
Would be together,
I thought that it
Would last forever.

You made me happy
In a joyful kind of way.
You helped me to
Survive day after day.

There came a time
Where faith got lost,
And due to unfortunate circumstances
There was an emotional cost.

Everything I said,
Believe me, it's true.
I did not lie
When I said that I love you.

There then came a time
That was strangely amazing,
There were transition periods
Whilst emotions were phasing.

I hoped that you
Would never leave me,
But I watched the blinding
Scene across humanity

Distractions were placed
We got torn apart,
But you will forever
Be in my heart.

Decision

Am I dreaming?
Or am I awake?
There are major decisions
That I must make,
I must continue this path
Because who knows what's at stake?
Creativity is my "Footpath Tool",
It's like my metaphorical garden rake.

What could be the answer?
To the questions that I wonder so?
I need to think hard
Because I honestly do not know.
I have multiple emotions
Which build up and grow,
And I must choose wisely
Which emotions I want to show.

I asked for help from the lord,
I swear that this is true.
Because a time came
Where I didn't know what to do.
I looked up to the skies,
It was ever so blue.
I prayed for an answer
I prayed to renew.

I made my decision,
But I don't know how.
Whatever the decision,
I must stand by it, for now.
Even if the rhymes
Could bring an immense "wow",
I could expand on continuity
And then your minds could blow.

So, you want to know
The best of me
I will write it all down
For the rest to see.
I'll sit in my vest by a tree,
I'll expand my chest and show who's "blessed, to-be".
And I'll explain that there could
Be a true destiny.

Harmony

Each time that I
Pick up a pen,
And write another poem
Again, and again.
A time comes to my memory
But I cannot remember when,
A time when knowledge
Was beginning to stem.

Poem by poem,
Page by page,
I keep on moving
Up the stage,
I hold on to positivity,
I delete all my rage.
Even though I cannot
Earn a decent wage.

I write rhymes and I rap
I sing songs, I get mad,
Yes, there are times
Where I'm feeling sad.
But time moves on,
And for this, I'm truly glad.
Even though I will cherish
All the good things we had.

Not many know the truth
Of whom I am today,
It's hard to describe
What I'm supposed to say.
But I'll try to find a way
With the word games that I play
Because I like to keep it random
When things get handed on my tray.

It's hard to explain the truth
When tears start to fall
Because emotions can overtake rationality
And halt the "game of ball".
Especially when there are obstacles
Which stop us feeling tall.
They like to interfere from the outside,
They try to make us small.

The positive vibe
Which can be found,
Is not hard to find
When you listen to the sound,
Just look at the beauty,
That's scattered all around
And life can switch
In a harmonious rebound.

Today & Tomorrow

Light the candles,
Eat the cake,
Treat yourself
To a chocolate flake.

Your day has come,
You're forty-four today.
It's time to celebrate,
What more can I say?

Put on your makeup,
And dye your hair.
You make a mess
Everywhere.

You go out
And get paralytic,
You won't even care
If you look pathetic.

You get home,
It's now time for bed,
This time tomorrow,
You'll forget all that you've said.

Wash off your smudged makeup
From when you had your fun.
No, wait! Leave it on…
…or you'll scare everyone!

So Called

People fall in love
So, they say.
Well, what is love?
Is it a game that we play?

Does love exist?
No, take my advice.
I thought I was in love,
But I had to think twice.

It lasted five years
And then I found out
That it wasn't meant to be,
The plans got thrown about.

Love's a so called "game",
We all take chances,
What are these
So called "romances"?

Try not to get hurt,
It's a waste of time.
This isn't being selfish,
It's not a so called "crime".

I try not to fall
Into the heartbreak trap again,
Because I'm aware of the inflicted
Indescribable pain.

Live each moment
The best way that you can,
Save your love for humanity
And you'll be a much smarter man.

Live your own life
Do not get pulled down.
Be the ruler of your world,
Be a king without a crown.

Save your heart
For that angel from above,
For that angel, you must care for,
For that angel, you must love.

The Magic Way

Is this your card?
Is this card right?
I sit and I practice
My magic tricks each night?

Trick after trick,
Show after show,
You don't know what it feels like
To hear the audience say "wow".

I love magic,
This is true,
It's one of the activities
That I like to do.

Ii will never give up
My magic, never.
Magic is in my blood
Both now and forever.

I practice each day,
What more is there to say?
Nothing else except
Magic is my way.

Finest

Why must the Earth
Seem so unfair?
Why must people act
As if they don't care.

They don't understand
As I offer my hand
In a gesture with no resistance.
I once got pulled down
And I lost my crown
I realised I needed assistance.

I went on my path
To escape an evil wrath.
I battled the demons inside.
No matter how far I would run
In the light of the sun,
I knew I had no place to hide.

I never knew how well
I needed to hide behind
The invisible curtain
When I was truly blind.

With no place to go
And no place to know
Where my answers could be found.
So, I fell to the floor,
It felt like a war.
I just laid there on the ground.

I awoke from my hell,
I heard the "gong" of the church bell,
I once again started to be me.
I pulled myself up,
I gripped the ceramic cup
And poured the finest tea.

Angel (Part I)

Is this my life?
Is all of this happening?
Is all this true?
Is this the real thing?

For the last few months,
I've experienced something new,
My life became different
I knew not what to do.

Someone was sent down,
They must have come from heaven,
I felt the synchronicities begin
When I stared at the number eleven.

I tried to stop it,
I almost rang a bell,
I almost pushed up daisies
Which were planted deep in hell.

I used to be upset,
Not many people could tell,
But not I've been blessed
By a guardian angel.

I see that this angel
Has now entered my life,
Before this angel,
Nobody tried to remove the knife.

This angel means
So much to me
Without the angel, I'd be lost.
I hope that you can see.

Free Falling (Part I)

What I believe,
What I feel,
It's all so amazing,
It cannot be real.

First, we hugged,
It couldn't be missed.
Then to my amazement
We kissed.

Let me ask something,
"What is this?"
There was an entire night
Where the snake couldn't hiss.

Everything I say,
Can you see that it's true?
It's even truthful when I say
I'm free falling for you

Thanks to You

I'm getting up on the right side of the bed,
Thoughts are racing through my head.
I can't stop thinking about what you said,
I sometimes feel shy and my cheeks will turn red.

I know I feel a lot for you,
I'm finally thinking things which must be true.
Without a thought of sadness or feeling blue,
All these new emotions are now thanks to you.

Thanks to you, I feel so bright,
Thanks to you, I've seen the light,
Thanks to you, I have something to write
Thanks to you, I can sleep at night.

I just wish I could put things in words that I can say,
I wish I could tell you the truth I feel today,
I wish I could tell you but there isn't a single way
When I describe the things I'm feeling, it's like a love-game that we play.

The neurons within myself has changed its thinking plan,
I now feel more confident, because I know that I can.
I feel like I've cooled down without the use of a fan,
This supernatural volcano has erupted and emerged a new superman.

When I first saw you, I set a pace,
But my mind is now moving all over the place.
I'm no longer living slowly. I'm now ahead of the race.
I now see the truth each time I see your face.

A Random Birthday

You're getting older
Through every single day
Look at your hair,
You've started going grey.

For your age,
You are really fit,
But you comb your hair…
…Well, what's left of it.

Now you're slowing
Down your pace.
You see the wrinkles
Growing on your face.

Maybe later
You could go for a drive,
Now, calm down because
You're only forty-five.

Now get ready to go out,
You chose what to wear,
This item may help you…
…It's dye for your hair.

The Man

He has blue eyes,
He has brown hair,
It sometimes seems quiet,
I swear, he'll never swear.

He wears a watch
But he's unaware of the time,
He acts like a "goody-goody",
He doesn't commit a crime.

He wears trousers
That is too big,
He's so thin and tall,
He has the figure of a twig.

I look at his feet,
I see he has "old man shoes",
You'll never see this sober man
Going out to drink booze.

I look at his arm,
I see three buttons on his sleeve,
Who is this man?
Well, his name is Steve!

Angel (Part II)

I look to the sky,
What do I see?
I see starts shining
As they are winking at me.

At night when it's cool,
I sit and I look
At the beautiful stars
Whilst reading a book.

It's soothing and relaxing,
Especially when it's quiet.
I love how it feels,
It's the opposite of a riot.

The night is soothing,
The whole world's asleep,
It makes me emotional,
I cry and I weep.

I start to think
About a lot of things
Like a team of angels
With everlasting wings.

That's How

One, two, three,
How is thee?

Zero, one, two,
How are you?

Seven, eight, nine,
Are you fine?

Eight, nine, ten,
I won't ask again.

Two, one, half,
There's no need to laugh.

Four, five, six,
Things begin to fix.

The Honest Truth

Thank you for being
So loving and kind,
You've been there for me
Without changing your mind.

The truth is that you
Are truly number one,
If you ever need me,
I'll help you if I can.

I want to spend
The rest of my life
With you forever,
Husband and wife.

With your gentle touch,
With your beautiful face,
We both seem to be
In the same mental place.

I enjoy spending
My time with you,
It's the kind of thing
That I love to do.

I love to communicate
Whilst holding your hand,
I'll even cherish your hair,
Yes, every strand.

With your silky soft skin
And your beautiful smile,
If I was to ever lose you,
I'd search every mile.

Each day I realise
That I'm yours and you're mine.
I love it when we watch films,
Even though we don't drink wine.

You may get angry, I may get stroppy,
But we're both alike.
If I didn't feel this way,
I'd probably take a hike.

But enough of that,
From the old and into the new,
The truth is
I have real feelings for you.

Pulling Through (Part I)

I'm sitting here wondering
Which stage I could be at.
I have issues in the past,
But I try not to think of that.

A straight edge lifestyle,
No alcohol or drug,
No feeling like an addict,
No feeling like a thug.

I have clean blood flowing
My pure mind thinks,
But there is tobacco in my rollups
And Pepsi in my drinks.

There are voices of temptations,
There are voices of unknown,
There are voices I can control,
There are voices that have grown.

There are voices that cannot be ignored,
There are voices that cannot be put aside,
There are voices that makes me
No longer want to hide.

I live my own life,
I'm the boss of me,
I control my own life,
I control my destiny.

What matters not;
Are the voices in my head.
It's sometimes irrelevant
What the nasty voices said.

I chose what's true,
Yes, me. Not you.
What else can I do?
I'm already pulling through.

Task

This poem could be garbage,
But what would you expect?
It cannot be great
Because it's just a school project.

This task could probably
Keep me up all night,
Mainly because
I know not what to write.

You see the struggle
Verse after verse,
You can sense this curse
Is getting worse.

Now that I
Know not what to say,
I decide I want to
Enjoy the outside today.

I want to socialise,
So, people can be befriended.
Well, now I can,
Because this poem has ended.

Bag Made by Lidl

The possibilities are endless,
What could be inside?
Is it a place where creepy crawlies
Gather together to hide?

Is it a place where secrets are kept?
Is it a place where things cannot be seen?
Is it a place to keep shampoo?
And other things that are clean?

It will hold things,
Both heavy and light,
It sits in front of us
Hiding in plain sight.

Does it contain a music piece?
Like a well treated fiddle.
I guess I'll never know
What's inside the bag made by Lidl.

Us

I felt love,
When you entered my life.
The time then came
When I thought that you'd be my wife.

I thought you were the one
That was sent from above,
I thought you were the one
Because what I felt was love.

You were the one
That I wanted to see
Lying in my arms,
Just you and me.

To find someone like you
It was the luck of the draw,
Because to find someone like you,
It was like an angel that I saw.

Facebook

It's blue coloured background,
The things people write,
Some people stay up
Writing messages during the night.

Posting pictures and their thoughts
Whilst explaining how they feel,
Not knowing what feed is false
And whether the false news is real.

Life stories and explanations
Describing what they think,
Despite the awfulness of the black mirror,
I read the positivity, and then I blink.

Before I continue to write a post of my own
To explain the things that I see
I explain that my thoughts have grown.
Then I say things that cannot be.

I set goals and objectives,
I study the things that I read,
Then I share the things that's worth reading
Across the blue news feed.

Starting New (Part I)

I cannot tell if I'm upset
Despite the things that I had,
There was a time that I fell in love,
And for this I'm truly glad.

My friends were weird, they wouldn't talk
I was left all alone, you see?
They won't share their feelings
And it's rather uncomforting to my glee.

I cannot stand the feeling
Of depression anymore,
I cannot stand the feeling
Of my wrists being sore.

I wish I understood
Why I felt that we belonged,
I listen to my music,
And hope that nobody is being "wronged".

I ignore all the issues,
They begin to end right now,
I move away, I start anew,
And then I tell you how.

The One

I'm sitting here,
After a new lesson,
Thinking of everything
The journey's begun.

I fall in love when I see
People with their smile.
I share these feelings
Every once and a while.

I'm sitting alone
With something exciting to do
I'm thinking about things
That helps me pull through.

I travel many miles,
Searching for a place to be.
I finally find a home,
Despite the things that I see.

I miss the past.
There are memories that can touch
Me in the heart.
And I miss them so much.

I cannot help but think
About things that shouldn't be
Like "the point of perspective",
Which is something that we see.

I say the things that I say
Because I feel that it is true,
I walk the path that I walk
Because it shows me what to do.

I listen around, I absorb the ambience,
I make myself at home,
Because when happiness surrounds, we sit on the ground
And peacefulness becomes the norm.

Terminator

You can't hear him,
His silence will speak.
The lack of sound is deafening
From week to week.

His shirt is blue,
His eyes will glare,
He squints and looks over,
To my surprise, he'll stare.

He starts to yell
In our face,
He threatens to throw us
Around the place.

He sits in his chair
With his blank expression.
He's silently happy,
And he'll thank depression.

His clothes are cheap,
He has a red jacket,
He threatens to his us
With a tennis racket.

I wouldn't be surprised
If he wore sunglasses which were black,
It doesn't matter if he leaves us,
Because he'll say, "I'll be back".

Super Sis (Part II)

Dear Tonia,
There's no debate
That you, my sister
Are just great.

It comes again,
The end of May,
It's now your
Twenty-third birthday.

You should enjoy yourself,
Go out and have fun.
You should have a party
With everyone.

You drink some wine,
Sip by sip.
But be careful,
I have a top tip.

I hope you get everything
That's on your birthday list.
So, here's Tommy's Top Tip…
…Don't get p*ssed!

Caswallon

What can I do?
What can I say?
I found the silliest
Name ever, today.

I don't even know how
To pronounce it correctly,
But I'll try,
In case you respect me.

It's an awesome name,
One that I truly adore,
I love weird names,
I need to find more.

There are many names,
Like Steve, Bob and John.
But this name is unique,
It's called "Caswallon".

A Random Day

Make a wish,
Eat a fish,
Run around slowly
With a chocolate dish.

I slip on ice,
It isn't nice,
Take your time
When you chase mice.

There's a fox on fire,
The smoke rises higher.
It's shaped like a duck,
What the f*ck?

Pulling Through (Part II)

I feel hate,
There's no debate,
I lost my chance,
It's much too late.

It's not meant to be,
Both you and me.
You made your choice,
Can't you see?

I had my chance,
I took my last glance,
I guess we won't have
That feeling of romance.

I'm feeling blue
Because of you,
I share these feelings
Because they're all true.

Don't you understand?
I wanted to hold your hand.
But I will snap back because
I'm like a rubber band.

You made me feel pain,
It drove me insane,
There were days where I wanted
To walk in the rain.

I couldn't escape my emotions, you see?
I wanted to break free
Because I knew deeply inside
That some of the feelings wasn't even me.

I inhale, and then I see a cloud as I puff,
The reasons for this include me having enough
Of day to day experiences
As well as other stuff.

My life got set off-track,
I will find my way back,
I'll do the things I do
Like a peaceful love attack.

Due to this twist of fate,
There's no debate
That I can pull through the other side
Without being in a terrible state.

My mind rings a bell,
I hope you can tell
That I'm moving on from problems
Because your lies don't sell.

Day

There's been a battle,
But the war isn't far.
The memories planted into my mind
Has left a permanent scar.

The battle may be over
But the war has just begun.
The war of peace holds such beauty,
We must win this one.

The enemy must fall
Because of the interference in the life that we live.
The war will then be over,
It's what I must give.

He stuck his feelings in my head,
There were things I couldn't tell,
Because along came the memory
Of getting lower as I fell.

This time, we must finish
The job which has been started.
And reconnect the missing pieces
Which once became parted.

This time, it's over,
He claims he has my back,
But I know that he's waiting there
Because he wants to attack.

Childhood

What is childhood? Is it a time for fun?
What is childhood? Is it a time to play with everyone?
Is it a time with humour? Is it a time with joy?
Is it a time to be happy to be a girl or a boy?

What is' childhood? It cannot be rotten,
What is childhood? It cannot be forgotten.
What is childhood? A fun time I had?
This I have not forgotten, and for this I'm truly glad.

Truth

People claim to hate me
But I know why.
It's because I claim
Life starts when I die.

It's the way that I act
Day after day,
But I'm just being myself
In every single way.

I'm just having a joke
And messing around.
There's no reason to beat me
Down to the ground.

I know you dislike me,
But there's no reason for it.
I don't care if my life
Beats me up a little bit.

I block out the pain,
I try to have some fun,
That's the reason that I wander
Around complimenting everyone.

I'm not seeking attention,
I just want to be a friend.
My problems can be serious
But I swear my fun doesn't end.

I will forever look
To seek what's true.
The stars and nature
Are the things that pull me through.

Remember the Mission (Part I)

When I write a rhyme,
I'm just explaining a time.
I think people need to listen,
You see? I'm on a mission.
I must say continuity, before it becomes forgotten,
I must mention memories, even though it may seem rotten.

I could go on forever,
Repeating the mistakes, but it isn't clever,
I'll talk about a quantum reality today
Because combining reality and fantasy
Is something that's hard to see.
Knowing reality is a state of mind
Whilst feeling the vibrations, the truth we'll find.

Combining material and spiritual, colliding emotions
Is something that could seriously cause some commotions.
Keeping happiness, positivity is how I feel
Because people start to learn that some things aren't real.
Some things become more real within the mind,
These are the things that people try to find.

So, before it's all over, truth of reality is right,
Truth of reality could keep them up all night.
We cannot help the things we wonder, you see?
Sometimes the words get inserted into me.
Interlinking dimensions, maybe I should stop?
Maybe I should continue? But I may go over the top.

Some of these rhymes of which I speak,
Will return in my memory, as the days become a week.
The weeks become a month, then a year, now I see
That time flies so quickly like a leaf blowing off a tree
We look out to the sunshine; we look out to the rain,
We pray for forgiveness through issues once again.

Deal

I can't deal with you
And knowing what you done,
Making me believe
That you were "The One".

I cannot deal with you
After how you treated me,
Putting thoughts in my head,
But it helped me to see

I cannot deal with you
After what you put me through?
I cannot deal with negativity,
It must be over, you know it's true.

Angel (Part III)

There's an angel
Of whom I care for, so much.
But I know it's impossible
For us to touch.

Her amazing sense of humour,
It makes me share smiles,
If I were to lose here,
I'd pray as I travel miles.

The sparkles in the air,
I catch them with my eye,
If darkness took over,
I'd protect her as she'd cry.

Her sense of purity
Is what catches my attention,
I feel I need to mention
That I get lost in a daydream dimension.

She looks into my eyes,
That's when I see
How important
Angels are to me.

That Teacher

As I walk inside
The classroom today,
I tremble as I
Not know what to say.

I wish I were home,
I want my bed,
I don't want an evil teacher,
But the love will conquer the dread.

This teacher is the reason
That I make myself bleed,
I try to heal myself,
But due to failure, I pray, and I plead.

Although there's not much
That I can physically do,
I must stop the pain
That they are putting me through.

Go away, negativity.
It's something that must say goodbye,
It's a hurtful truth
That stays within your eye.

The evil teacher
Thinks I'm scared
But it fears love,
That must be shared.

Sing Along

My head starts to swirl,
My thoughts start to curl,
I start to think about
A supernova girl.

My mind took over
When I lost my four-leaf clover,
I felt my heart was left behind
By someone who was a supernova.

My eyes go around,
As I listen to each sound.
Some thoughts get forgotten,
Other thoughts become found.

There's no way to immortalise
Feelings of such size,
There's no way to explain,
There's no way to compromise.

I sit back and I inhale,
Here's a story, here's a tale.
There may be some tastes,
But they taste so stale.

But fear no wrong,
Listen to that song.
Do not hesitate
To start to sing along.

In the Mind

Sitting here
Thinking of you
Is the kind of thing
That I like to do.

You look like a princess,
Your lovely long hair.
How can I explain
That I honestly do care?

The amazing stare
From your beautiful eyes,
Always take me
By surprise.

The way that you talk
Always makes me smile.
I haven't felt like this
In such a long while.

You are perfect
In every single way.
You help me get by
From day to day.

I could list forever
All the good things about you.
Every word
Would forever be true.

The Door

The weird wooden mystery
With wisdom within,
I never know
Who's going to walk in.

Who could walk through?
Let us wait and see,
The door can be exciting
For both you and me.

It's unusual knowledge,
What could be behind?
You may never know
What you could find.

When you walk through
The wooden frame,
Inside and outside,
It will never be the same.

It isn't made of metal,
It's not wooden, it's glass.
I wonder what it's in there
As I walk passed.

It's connects the outside
To what's on our floor.
I consistently am wondering
What's behind this door?

Feel

I've missed you,
I hope that you see,
I honestly love you,
And I hope that you believe me.

When we don't talk,
You're still in my head.
Even when it's hard
To remember the things that's said.

I want to remember
How I held you so tight,
I want you to stay with me
During the night.

I'll keep in contact,
I'll keep in touch.
I want you to know
That I love you so much.

I'll do anything to remember,
I plead and I cry,
Please don't be sad,
Share happiness in your eye.

I love when I remember
Things that was true,
I hope that you notice
That it's hard to learn what to do.

My Life

I walk around
I sometimes feel sly,
I feel like a bad guy
I feel I should lie.

I have plans within my head,
Ideas on what to do,
I don't want people to suffer,
I want to see this through.

We must eliminate the hard times,
We must ignore pain,
I don't want to be a nuisance,
It's not nice to feel insane.

We must share
All the positive emotions
I have a special feeling
That we can avoid commotions.

I control my life,
I feel I'm not free.
Negativity won't be
An issue to me.

Why?

I have many reasons
That circled in my life
As to why I'd grip tightly
Whilst holding a knife.

People made me
Feel quite bad,
It made me feel guilty
And it drove me mad.

Out of the people
That tackled me with wit,
I knew that one day
I would get through it.

Somebody once changed me,
I got ignored, as I did too.
I felt like I was crazy,
I didn't know my crew.

You became the reason
I felt empty inside
I didn't know where you were,
I didn't remember you could hide.

You helped me to change,
I hope that you see,
I just wish I knew why
This was happening to me.

Drink (Part I)

The taste is really soothing
As it drips on my tongue,
It reminds me of a soft song
That has been sung.

It tastes so amazing
On my parched dry lips,
I drink loads of it,
With thousands of sips.

It's warm and lovely,
I adore the taste,
I could drink it forever
Without it going to waste.

I could drown in the taste,
It's perfect for me.
What is this drink?
It's PG Tips, decaf tea.

Taken Away

Here we go,
I type once again,
I no longer live
My life in vain.

As I hold my cheap lighter
And light my cheap roll.
I allow my life
To take its toll.

I sit back and I look
Deep into my mind, with kindness.
I look at nothing,
Prayers balance the blindness.

Seeking freedom,
Seeking what's true,
Looking for an answer
Looking at the sky, which is blue.

A tree in the corner
The candle is lit,
On this black and blue armchair
Is where I must sit.

Why am I here?
I just cannot see,
The meaning of life
Is what concerns me.

Why can I move?
Is the sound I hear real?
Is the smell that arrives real?
How do we really feel?

I'll never stop looking
For these answers in my days,
Because it's better when there's light
On the subject for our walkways.

What I'm Willing to Do

I'm willing to fight
And stay up during the night
Battling with the demons
To make sure that we're alright.

I'll do anything for you,
I'll hold on to what's true,
To ensure that happiness
And love is what pulls through.

What will it be?
I cannot see,
Together forever,
Peace for everybody.

Together until the end,
I just follow this trend,
Because I swear the meaning behind all this
Will get disclosed by the end.

We all work together,
We ensure it lasts forever,
I beg and plead for truth,
I'm searching for whatever.

I know that each day
Things get in the way.
But I honestly feel love
For all the things that we can say.

To Lose

To lose the best thing that's ever happened to you,
To lose the only love that you felt was true.
To lose the only person that would make you smile,
To lose a person that you loved for such a while.

To lose your happiness to heartache that's bad,
To lose the only sense of happiness that you ever had.
To lose your faith in God and love,
To lose your reason to ask questions above.

To lose your feelings and lose your pride,
To lose your confidence this makes you want to hide.
To lose that person that you loved so much,
To lose memories of how you felt when you used to touch.

To lose that feeling of when it begun,
To lose that person who you thought was the one.
To lose the best thing that's ever happened to you,
To lose the only love that you felt was true.

Getting to Know Me

If you want to know
A little about me.
Let's get some things off my chest
So that you can see.

I'm not a perfect being,
I've done some rights and some wrongs.
I've had my fair share of unfairness,
And times where'd I'd cry to my favourite songs.

But try to keep a smile,
And for my friends I do care.
I want my family to know,
That I love you, I swear.

I may very well be boring you
With each of my failed rhymes,
Well arrest me if rhyming
Is committing any crimes.

If you want to get to know me,
If you want to speak again,
Mr T R Andrews@live.com,
Email has replaced my MSN.

There's one last thing
That I'd like to say,
Everybody out there…
…HAVE A NICE DAY!!

Chapter 2

Stepping Stones across the Tides

Introduction

My name is Tommy, no longer Matt.
This is the follow-up to "Footpath".
I've been through a lot since I wrote that.
I've been through all sorts of hell, some stories I won't tell
For all different reasons, some things I won't sell.
So, here's another random mix
Of rhyming stories to be told.
You will see a lifestyle, it'll begin to unfold.
Now then, my fellow people,
Keep learning what's true.
I'm inviting everybody,
That's including you.
What I said has been acknowledged,
Information's fed to you on a tray,
So, before I forget...
...HAVE A NICE DAY!!

Looking (Part I)

I don't look for fans,
It's just not for me,
Fans can just vanish
Like a leaf on a tree.

I don't look for money
In this silly old world
Because I'm too busy
To even look for a girl.

I don't look for fame
Because I don't like a crowd,
Also, because I
Don't like noise to be loud.

I don't look for alcohol,
I don't like to be drunk,
I may as well be straight edge
And become a monk.

I don't look for using
My friends from above,
I just look for happiness,
I just look for love.

Busy Railway Station

As I chain my blue bike to the motorcycle stands,
I walk past the people with cigarettes in their hands.
Taxis, Buses, Vans and Company Cars around,
I began to walk towards the door as I look down to the ground.

I walk past the shop, where people get their food and drink
And head towards the ticket barrier as I begin to think.
Cafe's, toilets and shops and vending machines, people everywhere.
All on separate travels, nobody seems to care.

The television-timetable which reads the time of the train,
People in thick jackets, just in case of any rain.
Security guards with handcuffs attached to their belt,
Ready to cuff any person without a ticket to be felt.

Information desks are swarmed by people who gather around like flies.
People meeting and leaving as they say their hellos and goodbyes.
I pace the corridor slowly towards the platform I must be,
To head towards the waiting room to wait for the train this will come for me.

Smells of oil, gas and coal in the atmosphere which does surround,
People yelling and screaming, everywhere there's sound.
I hear the voice on the tannoy that says the train will arrive,
Next to the window I will sit as the train begins to drive.

I glance out the window,
I think as I look to see,
And I ask myself the question,
What will this destination hold for me?

Bubbles (Part I)

You can buy a tube of bubbles in the UK
For around the price of ninety-nine pence.
Or if you're in the United States,
It'll be around One dollar and seventy-five cents.

You place the plastic circle
Inside the tube of fairy liquid.
Then you blow out some bubbles,
If you're under the age of ten, it's wicked!

Then again, even now
I sometimes want to just go
To buy myself some bubbles
And remember my childhood so.

So, what's the story of these bubbles?
What more about them can I say?
I know, I have decided!
I want a bubble machine for my birthday!

Drink (Part II)

People stumble
After drink,
They vomit in
The kitchen sink.

They stumble across
The passage hall,
They slip and tumble,
They begin to fall.

They throw up all
They ate that day,
They forget what they
Want to say.

To make it worse,
They start to cry,
They fall to the floor,
They yell at the sky.

They collapse and sleep
Falsely for an hour,
When they awake,
Their tongues will be sour.

They cannot control
How they feel,
They lose grip and forget
What is real.

Their brain cells die,
They cannot think,
All because of the
Alcoholic drink.

Some People (Part I)

There are some people in this world
That brings hell to earth,
There are some people in this world
That is evil from birth.

There are some people in this world
That causes destruction,
There are some people in this world
That blows up like a volcanic eruption.

There are some people in this world
That wants to hurt others around,
There are some people in this world
That laughs at those on the ground.

There are some people in this world
That will pick on you and me,
But there are some people in this world
That just wants everyone to be free.

Look for those people
Your life has begun,
Stay with the light, even at night
And you'll defeat the other one.

A Time before (Part I)

Some friends in my life
That I miss,
Some happy memories
Feel like bliss.

Male and female friends
Who left footprints in my life,
Honest and true friends
Who took away the knife.

Real decent people
Who've always been there,
People who've showed me
That they will always care.

A real-life story
That sticks in my mind,
A deceiving lie
That keeps the truth blind.

Loving warm relationships
Between my friends and I,
Both sad and happy memories
They force me to cry.

But through it all
I've come to see,
How much these people
Mean to me.

Love and peace
Is felt forever, always,
I will care for these
Until the rest of my days.

My Associates

My eyes are opening today,
I see what I'm supposed to see,
A little something to the ones
Who are always there for me.

To the two who made me fall,
It's truly "same old sh*t",
Both times was an experience
But I have learned from it.

Some friends, we have drifted apart,
My two best friends from school.
We should all meet up more,
You're both to me, still cool.

My associates at work,
Like a little family team,
That will always stick together,
We understand what we mean.

I have family who is
Always in my mind.
But I no longer wake up
Feeling un-dead, feeling blind.

I thank everybody that has ever
Been there for me throughout.
The pain and the problems experienced,
Some know what I'm talking about.

Things may be difficult
For me to explain each day,
All my greatest associates,
I'm here for you always.

I'll do what I can to hold on
To what is important to me
And I'll inhale the truth around,
I will sometimes need some help, you see?

I'll do what I can,
I will stick to what I see,
I'll try to always
Be myself and be free.

Reclusive

I block out the humans,
I hide all my feelings,
I ignore all my problems,
I have nothing to believe in.

I jump to conclusions,
I hide my expressions,
I take a detour,
In different directions.

I forget where I'm going,
I forget where I came from,
I know not of my heritage,
Where do I belong?

I read people's faces,
I work out their thought plan,
I enjoy my relaxation,
Whilst learning of the man.

I know it's not real,
This visual delusion,
Its interference,
This personal intrusion.

I hide in the corner,
I listen around me,
I hide what I'm feeling
So, people cannot see.

I know there's an exit,
Same place as the entrance,
So, I put one foot by the other
In a fighting stance.

Helping Decision of the Beaver

You begin to step off the plane,
What do you begin to see?
In the skip, a broken table
Which is as brown as brown can be.

Take a step towards this item,
Now stop and scratch your lip,
Because you'll be ever so shocked
When you look inside this skip.

Behind this table, nestled motionless,
A poor beaver has passed,
He must have got sick, that must suck,
He is painless now at last.

You turn around, take a step
And re-board the high-fly plane.
Australia is too far, Canada's at a par.
It's enough to drive the pilot insane.

Parallel Shift

Synchronicity,
Numbers repeat,
Letting you know
That you are walking your beat.

The dreams of past memories
That you remember at night,
They trigger that memory
In your brain with delight.

Mountains and trees
In your explorations,
Triggering memories
That exceeds your expectations.

Signals of being
And what you feel is true,
Feelings of emotions
And remembering what to do.

Learning your true self,
Remembering your name,
Bad habits will vanish,
Things will not feel the same.

True feelings, true knowing
Within this reality experience,
Exploring the corridors
Without security clearance.

The rainbow of oneness,
The materialistic creation choice,
The vision of our mission,
You hear it in your voice.

Remember our past,
Remember our life,
Remember our being
Before we're at strife.

With mistakes, we can rectify,
Remember what brought us here
Remember with harmony,
We'll succeed without fear.

Awake from the illusion
That's been pulled before our eyes,
The memories of machines
That took us by surprise.

Fear when placed
In captive pods,
Alongside people
We are now like Matrix mods.

But we see and feel the glitches
From time to time.
We doubt our integrity,
Replacing bravery with crime.

Pods filled with blackness,
The Oxygen within the holes
Human crossed with mech-madness,
They're trying to take our souls.

Fight the falseness within your mind,
Remember from where you came,
Fight the evil from the demonic invasion,
Suddenly realities aren't the same.

From dreams to memories
To calmness with fear,
Repairing a soul
That has been trapped here.

Do what we must,
Living side by side,
Looking to that corner
Where you know they hide.

Stay positive stay true,
Know who you must be,
Looking into this world
Still trying to be free.

Looking back at a memory
That no longer seems to be,
Living a life whilst remembering
That conscious connecting tree.

Artificial deception,
I know not from when I came,
All I'm sure is now is
Things no longer feel the same.

"You have a mother and she loves you"
A voice in my head says softly within
Leaving one world into another
Once again, we will begin.

A spiritual memory
Of a past about where we live
What is our mission? Why are we here?
What are we supposed to give?

Red lights, eye scanners,
Some people shall not pass,
Mass gatherings, mass illusions,
Invasion and trespass.

Remember your direction, remember your dreams,
Remember from where you came,
Remember your correction, remember your screams,
Things do not feel the same.

Remember the chambers, remember the lasers,
Remember the crumbling walls,
Remember the robots, remember the liquid,
Remember what's behind their curtain poles...

Wind entering, like a dimensional vortex,
Spirituality combined with movement,
Continue the journey, know your intentions,
Remember for your own improvement.

Kicked by a Hammer

In the backstreet of London
Is where it begun,
Drug dealers, alcoholics,
Caffeine addicts having fun.

Rats run along,
Drains create a stench,
But there's a rusty old hammer
Lying on the bench.

You may use the hammer
To break locks to the zoo,
But don't anger the animals,
Or you'll get kicked by a kangaroo.

Different Year

Every year, at my place
You see the smile on my face,
Another year, no special day,
But I feel happy in a different way.

Every year, something's not right,
Something fills my eyes with fright.
I get upset, then I cry,
Nobody knows why and neither do I.

I feel as if there's something wrong,
Something that's been missing all along.
There's an empty space inside of me,
Every year, I feel unhappy.

But this year... It's different though.
My empty space is empty no more,
Someone filled it from above,
It's been filled with something that's called love.

I've never had this feeling so,
Not last year or the year before.
This year I have a feeling, I hope that you know...
...I've been filled with light, which beams a bright glow.

Happiness

Happiness is a feeling,
When your smile is true.
Happiness is a feeling,
When you don't feel blue.

Happiness is shown
From a loved one to a friend.
Happiness is an emotion
That drives me around the bend.

Happiness is a thought,
That sticks in your mind.
It causes friendliness,
To show love and be kind.

It's a feeling you show,
When you are not sad,
It balances you out
And it stops you from going mad.

These are ways
To describe that "happiness" word,
But to ask what is happiness?
May sound obscured.

Nobody knows how to
Explain what it means.
But there is an answer,
Hidden in dreams.

One Day

One day, you may see it,
One day, you won't.
One day, you want it,
One day, you don't.

One day, you are happy,
One day, you are sad.
One day you're excited,
One day, you feel mad.

One day you are silent,
One day, you are loud.
One day, you are focused,
Then you're floating with the clouds.

Single vision, blurred vision,
Double then scramble,
Travel your mind,
Thought plan unravel.

See pictures, see people,
Almost like a daydream,
But you know it's all real,
You can't hold in your scream.

Something will stick,
In your everyday duty,
Just look for the glory
And look for the beauty.

One More Step

I hear the voices, I follow.
I live my life, so hollow.
I live a life of sorrow.
"Happiness" I wish I could borrow.

I wake up in the morning,
Or more like the afternoon.
I look around for love,
A love that was lost so soon.

I care for each person,
I try to show all love,
But it's hard to feel emotions
Whilst praying to above.

It's hard to do the right thing
When it's impossible to do.
But when you got a hand to hold,
You know that you'll pull through.

For those who has no hand
To hold throughout the night,
Just know that you can survive,
You know you'll have to fight.

Maybe not with violence,
Not with anger, but with emotion.
Just follow your life through,
Live each day through all the commotions.

Pass the test; get an "A",
Do the best that you can,
Live your life; just do your best,
You can be a superman.

If you feel like you failed,
Take a step; think about who you are,
Start again, take one more step.
And walk quite far.

Mothers Day

I wanted to write
My mother a song,
But I cannot write songs,
They always go wrong.

So instead here's a poem
To you, from me.
A poem to show you
What I'd like you to see.

The truth is, I'm grateful
For all that you've done,
As a mother to us,
You're truly number one.

You're a supermom, a super-nana,
And a role model to follow,
Without you in our lives,
Our hearts would be hollow.

All that I'm saying is that
All this is true.
One more thing,
Happy Mother's Day to You.

Smile

I don't know how
To express my feelings,
I don't know how
To talk to other beings.

I don't know how
To explain my mind,
I block out my thoughts
To try to be kind.

All I ever wanted
Was to do the right thing,
All I ever wanted
Was to be happy as I sing.

I just want to see
Other people smile,
But I cannot smile myself,
It's been such a while.

I turn my head
And force it to be
I make the smile happen
It tricks the brain, you see?

When you feel down
Remember what you must do,
Force the smile, despite your feelings,
You will find that you'll pull through.

Coin Flip

Flip the coin,
Heads or tails,
Make a plan
That never fails.

Jump the hoop,
The hurdle, then run.
Whilst wearing black sunglasses
To protect us from the sun.

Don't touch the bugs,
The sickness has spread,
So, live your life with glory
And not in sorrow or dread.

Show the right example,
Show us the good that lurks inside.
Show us the truth of all the answers,
So, we won't ever have to hide.

Do you see the dark rift?
See passed the dimensional shift,
Our visions of happenings
Has began to slowly drift,

Watch the world lift
Believe in your gift.
If you see your mind begin to drift,
Be careful you don't get miffed.

If you feel the negativity
On the heads side of the quid,
Flip over to positivity,
Negativity, we've just got rid.

Collectables

Personal items,
Things I collect,
Rings and wristbands too,
Items of clothing,
Things I find soothing.
Things that pull me through.

The meditation stones,
The guardian angel,
That my granny left for me.
The Zippo lighter,
Fridge magnets and key rings
They are what help me to see.

There's life beyond
These four walls,
You just got to get out and explore.
Just follow your footpath,
Leave your own footprints
Speed walking across the floor.

Memories and collectables,
Things that you gather,
Those materialistic gems.
One day you'll learn
To finally turn,
You'll know you don't need them.

When that happens,
And sales all fall
And the hypnosis doesn't work,
They push obvious fakery
To keep us in slavery,
They attempt to drive us bezerk.

Now they see,
The transformation
It's explained within this rhyme.
It's in the open,
Our words have been spoken,
It's now just a matter of time.

Earth (Part I)

We've used Gods gifts
For our own personal use,
We've built on this world
With concrete abuse.

The hills have been covered
With tarmac so black,
To cover the grass
That will never grow back.

We've polluted the air
With petrol and gas
We've destroyed our own home,
It happened so fast.

We've broken the ozone
With our own selfishness,
We ignore all the problems
We carry on with no fuss.

When God will return
To reclaim his land
He'll destroy us all
With the use of one hand.

Looking back after learning,
The ozone, no more.
He didn't destroy us,
Just the reality would go.

Our conscious just shifted
Somewhere, elsewhere
People just questioned
"Was this shift fair?"

Maybe it's necessary
In order to save
The soul of light
From becoming a dark slave.

The location adjustment,
The differences between
The different worlds
And all that's in between.

The near-death memories
When your mind was elsewhere
Memories erased
In order to make it fair.

Remember there's a reason
That we must look after where we live.
What are we to do, if earth couldn't pull through?
And it had nothing left to give?

What Have I Done?

What have I done?
I cannot believe.
What have I done?
I can't help but grieve.

What have I done?
I think I've messed up.
What have I done?
I cannot put up.

What have I done?
I feel like a fool.
What have I done?
It reminds me of school.

What have I done?
I just don't feel right.
What have I done?
I feel like I've ruined my night.

What have I done?
I just don't know.
What have I done?
I just want to go.

What have I done?
What have I begun?
What shall I do?
What have I done?

Fate

There are thoughts that race
Throughout my head,
There are dreams I see
As I sleep in my bed.

There are things I see
That make me feel
Like I'm unsure
Of what is real.

There are times I zone out
And go to my own little place,
There are times I show no
Emotions on my face.

There are times when time
Races by so quickly,
There are thoughts that make me
Feel ever so sickly.

There are times I feel
Like I'm not here,
There are feelings I get
Like frustration and fear.

But despite the thoughts
Of anger and hate,
I must question myself...
What is my fate?

Feelings

I feel like I'm moving on
Maybe getting somewhere,
I feel like I understand
The reason why I blankly stare.

I feel like I got the answer
That I've wondered for so long,
I feel like I know why
I'd get obsessed with certain songs.

I feel like I've got the answer
To why I find addictions hard,
I feel like now I know
Why my wrists were scarred.

I feel like the things I thought
Have all been in my head,
I feel like I must start new
My old life I must shred.

I feel like I asked for help
And it has finally arrived,
I feel like I have a new reason
To want to be alive.

Type of Life

Times get hard, times get tough,
Times you feel like you've had enough.
You try to answer those questions inside,
You try to feel normal, you try not to hide.

You wonder if those thoughts are meant to be,
You look at those images you can't help but see.
No force on the plane to help you escape,
No hero to save you, no mask and no cape.

No medicine, no items, no government help,
Sit down, scream and shout, then bellow and yelp.
No release, no freedom, locked away with a key.
No chainsaw to break through, to let loose and be free.

Trapped like a slave, being whipped in your mind.
These lies in the world that is keeping us blind.
Unable to help, unable to give.
That can't be the type of life you want to live.

Technology

Don't you find it ironic?
With all the technology produced,
All different gadgets
That is introduced.

Televisions and mobiles,
Computers and games,
Companies and trademarks,
With all different names.

PlayStation and Xbox,
And a Nintendo Wii
But these things are distractions,
That prevents us from being free.

The items in circulation,
That is worthless, really.
There are all different things
That costs money, you see?

Money has become everything,
It's unfortunate to say,
But if people had no money,
They couldn't survive the day.

Without following the system
That is created for us,
We would not have gadgets
Or cars, trains or a bus.

Advantages and opposes,
Both good and bad.
But it's not all good
For scepticism, be glad!

A Place to Go

There's a place
That you go
To clear your head.
A place
For freedom
Away from your bed.

There's a place
That you go
To put things alright.
A place
To escape
Through both day and night.

There's a place
That you go
A place to break free.
A place that's
A getaway,
It helps you to see.

There's a place
That you go
To get free from sin.
That place is in your mind
You need to
Just walk in.

Sudoku

You open the book
And look at the square,
Nine numbers across and down,
You begin to stare.

You begin to zone out,
And get lost in the mood,
Your mind gets occupied,
You forget about food.

You start to calculate
Which numbers goes where?
You get lost in the moment,
You're glued to your chair.

You fill in blank spots,
You focus your head,
You continue the puzzle
Whilst lying in bed.

You place the last number,
That number is Two,
What is this puzzle?
It's Sudoku.

Walking

He walks through the door,
Out into the rain.
It streams down the pavement,
Into the drain.

The birds and the creatures,
All soaking wet.
He struggles to light,
His damp cigarette.

He walks down the pavement,
And crosses the tarmac.
He passes the park
Whilst eating a Caramac.

He walks up the lane,
Past the old graveyard.
He walks to hide
His emotions that's scarred.

His aimless journey,
Takes him so far.
He continues his path,
With no need for a car.

He stops off half way,
To see an old friend.
Little does he know,
He's gone around the bend.

Before he realises,
How far he walked,
He picks up his phone,
To use the torch.

Four days later
He begins to smile.
When he realises
He's walked over a hundred miles.

True Story

Brainwave interception,
Mind play interrogation,
You'll see the moulting lava
Sweep across the nation.

Some truth will be shown,
Promises will be broken,
You may want to hide,
These demons have awoken.

Hide behind the sofa,
Or in the closet, you are trapped.
Make sure your life plans
Are re-planned, not scrapped.

Run through fire, walk on coal,
The beast's not far behind.
Look to the left then to the right,
You'd be surprised what you'd find.

Golden emblems, silver medals,
Coins to feed the poor,
Petrol shortage, neglect to all,
This story couldn't get any truer.

Travel

Jump up with your legs,
Throw on your motorbike boots,
Trek through the earth
Through the mucky roots

Travel the land,
Roll the dice,
Go where you must go.
Walk the roads,
Jump the hoops,
Distractions, just say no.

Drive right in,
Be free from sin,
Do well at every point.
Do the right thing,
Spread your wings,
Is that smoke from a cannabis joint?

Rain will rumble,
Thunder will tumble,
Making earthquakes across the globe.
The bombing sounds
That shatters around,
Fork lightning flashes
Across the ground.

The reasons beyond are deeper,
Much deeper, you wouldn't know...
...or do you already?
How much knowledge do you want to show?

What He Does

A voice will enter
And talk to my ears,
And tell me what to do.
He scares me, he worries me,
He confuses my head,
I don't know how to pull through.

He guides me through
Every single day,
He instructs me, he will teach,
We walk side by side,
Even when I try to hide,
Even when I lay on the beach.

He whispers soft words
He gives me signs
His rules, I must follow.
He gives me a knife
To end my life.
He makes me feel hollow.

He is my boss,
He is my leader,
He guides me through the day.
He gives me advice,
It's not always nice,
But he only wants to play.

If you know
That he's real,
Please know you can avoid
Hands together,
Truth forever,
Know that peace can fill that void.

Words

Words of violence
Are sometimes used.
Maybe not physically,
But verbally abused.

Words of happiness
Can cheer your mood,
They can comfort your feelings
While you're eating your food.

Words of hatred
Can cause some pain,
They can be enough to drive
A person insane.

Words of wisdom
Can help guide you through
Your life when it's tough
When you know not what to do.

There's one more word to mention,
Each time you look above,
The verbal fourth dimension,
This word is called love.

Friends

It's not that I don't love my friends,
I want to keep them until the end.
But they are sometimes too much for me,
They are overpowering, but they don't see.

They get so loud, it hurts my head,
They make me want to go to bed.
I don't want to lose them, of course,
I just feel like they're too close.

I feel like sometimes they don't think,
But I'd do anything for them before I could blink.
So, what can I do to not hurt them?
They to me are like a precious gem.

I just need alone time to focus my thoughts,
If I break any rules, I may get caught.
So, what can I say to back them off?
Maybe pretend to be ill and fake a cough?

So, it's time for me to do my best
To take time out and have a rest
To ease my mind and find my way
My friends may be loud throughout the day.

So, what can I do from now on?
Maybe just relax with my favourite song.
It would drive me around the bend,
To know that I would lose my friends.

Bed Linen

I remember walking
Up the stairs,
I saw a plump man
With pure white hair.

I walked in the office,
I then gave a smile,
I enjoyed the interview,
And the job for a while.

But to clean bed linen
Five days a week,
It would drive me so nuts
I felt like a freak.

I had to escape,
I had to get out,
I had to break free,
I just had to shout.

Now I am free,
I must decide,
Will I now face the world?
Or continue to hide?

Who Minds?

Surroundings will absorb,
Atmosphere intake,
Don't make that mistake,
For goodness sake.

Don't speak a word,
The voice you must abide,
No longer need to hide,
Cycle to near-glide.

Follow frequent flow,
Some super seasons show,
Both kind and unkind,
But hey, I don't mind.

I hope that you can follow
The rhythm to this beat.
If you know what I'm talking about,
Tap along with your feet.

Inner-conscious, mind expand,
Memories slip back,
Please stay calm, sound the alarm,
Conquer the mind attack.

Radiation, gamma rays,
Microwavable tricks,
Dumbing down to lose a crown,
Smoking cancer-sticks.

See the deception, know it's blinding,
Wear your inner-shades, and see
The mass illusion, it's no delusion
Be who you're meant to be!

Inside

Not thinking, mind blank,
Under mind-loss attack.
Do these words really make sense?
Or are they all just whack?

Feeling guilty, feeling happy
At the very same time.
Helping coppers and being a criminal,
Being a goody-goody whilst committing a crime.

Always two sides
To the story in your head,
Two voices that cannot co-exist
As you try to sleep in bed.

Random dreams that mean so much
But unable to figure them out.
Waking you up, frighten your life,
You begin to sit up and shout.

Drink your Pepsi, take your sip,
Wonder about all that will be.
Lose your mind, what do you find?
What do you begin to see?

I Miss Her

When my eyes were closed,
I was asked to see
And visualise somewhere
That I wanted to be.

To picture a place
That makes me smile,
To think about somewhere
That I could travel by miles.

It's strange to think
Even though I would
Think about the person,
I just wish that I could.

Each word that was said
From one to another,
I'd give anything for her
To be my true lover.

She made me smile, she built me
For years before meeting,
It all became real
When we had our first greeting.

It felt unreal, so beautiful,
Everything about her,
I mean it when I say
She made my life stir.

Triple A

The Apple falls
From the branch so long.
Realising that this
Is a comfort song.

The apple that falls
Creates the epiphany
As it bounces from the head
And enters eternity.

A place that could mean
So much or so little,
A place to re-create.
But be careful as its brittle.

Just follow each footstep,
Where will you?
Get the seeds from the apple
And plant a whole new tree.

Dream~Catcher

So, I walk downstairs
I grab cotton and a card,
I grab some scissors,
This project is hard.

I wrap cotton around
The cardboard, it's bright,
It's a lovely purple,
It stands out in the light.

I make a fancy web
In the centre with beads.
I develop a technique,
To fulfil my needs.

I attach some feathers
To complete it before I scream,
I have finished the catcher
To catch my bad dreams.

Jungle Life

Life is a jungle,
Life is a maze,
Life is a sequence
In every phase.

Life is a symbol,
Life is a road,
Life is a collection
Of knowledge to hoard.

Life gives you the ability
To focus your mind,
Why not focus on
Not becoming blind?

The voices are real,
The others are there,
Sometimes they comfort,
Sometimes they scare.

Why can't we see
What's around us above?
Each twinkling star
With energy of love.

Don't get me wrong,
Hate exists, you cannot deny,
But you must overcome it
On behalf of the sky.

Know to be honest,
Know to be friendly,
Know to be good
So that others can see.

Illness

All that I'm doing
Is puzzles and writing,
I sleep through the daytime
And follow instructions at night.

I can't control what goes down
As ink flows from my pen,
I can't help repeating myself
Again, and Again.

They told me I'm unwell
They put me on pills,
They told me I'd get better,
They told me I'm Ill.

They told me they'd help me
Make the voices go away,
But no matter what they do,
The voices will stay.

Life feels unreal
Like a game or simulation,
I wish I could restart
My life with a recreation.

I want to be normal
Weather it's beautiful or rotten,
But these words must be written
Before they're forgotten.

Then the switch will be pressed
But manipulated so discreetly,
They've got good by now,
They clean up so neatly.

They have practiced in time-zones
Unknown to another,
Sirens and choppers
All watching each other.

Hyphens and magic,
Letters of strange,
Stay strong when things
Eventually change.

Want to Know

Want to know
How I feel?
Want to know
What is real?

Want to know
Where to go?
Want to know
How to say no?

Want to know
The meaning of life?
Want to know
Where is your wife?

Want to know
Why each day is new?
Want to know
What is true?

Want to know
Why all you've learned
Gets erased during dreams
Like photos you've burned?

Want to know
Why you cannot seem to remember
What happened two days ago,
Let alone last September.

So, you want to know
These answers, do you?
Well, here's news for you,
I do too!

Forever

Holding you frozen
To the ground,
Hearing these arguments
All around.

Managers' discretion,
Is all about interpretation.
You can't complain,
There'll be discrimination.

Five long weeks,
Minus two degrees.
They refuse to give us leave,
She will still refuse to please.

Why is she so evil?
We just do not know,
We should show her the majority,
We should all protest so.

But it's all mouth, no action,
We do not stick together,
Will we unite? The bait, will she bite?
Or will this last forever?

Unite our hands and stand together,
Destroy the evil with the good.
Sweat drips from glands, spread peace forever,
Like you know you should.

Restart

Your hand will click,
Your neck will ache,
Your thoughts will scatter
Your brain will bake.

Your bones will hurt,
Your nails will break,
You curse yourself,
"For goodness sake."

You blame your mind,
You blame your head,
You wish that you
Could escape your dread.

You run away,
You start brand new,
You try to find out
What is true.

You start to worry,
You start to fail,
You go back to the beginning
With a brand-new trail.

Believe

Magic, the illusion
That nobody believes.
The impression of impossible
That the mind won't believe.
To bring back the loved ones
That we will all grieve,
To believe in the impossible
And not be naive.

To focus the mind
On doing something unreal,
To focus your hands,
On something to feel.
To make such a deal,
It's hard to tell the difference
Between what's fake and what's real.

To fly over a kingdom,
To look down below,
To bare your own children,
To watch them all grow,
So, if I ask if you believe
In god, and you say no,
Well how can you believe
In humanity, so?

We all come from somewhere
You must realise that,
We all hit home runs,
With that that ole baseball bat,
When we run, we try
To do the right thing,
But not all of us know
Where to begin.

Real

Am I here?
Can I see what I see?
Are all the things around me real?
Or is it like a screen of a TV?

Is vision a fake illusion?
Set in front to hide the truth?
Is it all in the mind
When I hear a voice through a phone booth?

Is life a reality?
Or is it just a real mind-game?
Is it real when you feel love?
Or is it a test to test your shame?

How can you know what to believe
With all the different theories that exist?
Is the blood dripping real
When the wall collides with your fist?

When you run your life on auto-pilot,
When there's no control at all.
When you feel all happy and cheerful,
Is it real when you fall?

Free (Part II)

I do not like to listen
To an awful loud noise,
I do not mix well
With many girls or boys.

I do not like to
Be in a big crowd,
Even two people
Can be too loud.

I do not like to
Feel like I'm confined,
But I like to know that I can
Come back to free my mind.

I don't like to be hidden,
I don't like to be open,
I don't like to be quiet,
But I fear the words that are spoken.

I hold close the things
That comforts me,
I just want to escape,
Please let me be free.

Earth (Part II)

Each living creature
Has a purpose of its own,
Each animal, every insect,
Look how they've grown.

They adapt, they survive,
Why can't we do the same?
Instead, we kill trees and creatures,
Yes, we humans are to blame.

It's stupid when you think,
How we've destroyed this Earth,
We are all brainwashed
From the day your mother gave birth.

We are brought up to know no different,
We learn as we grow up,
That we are the ones that ruined it all.
Just think about it next time you drink coffee from your cup.

But due to MK Ultra
And mind-manipulating materials,
Like coco pops on a pyramid,
We're not the killers, the elite are the serials.

This poem is supposed to offend if you oppose
And think that you can do
Whatever you like to hurt our home.
Stop hurting us, you know what to do.

With modern day advances, zero energy,
There's no reason for gas and oil,
Stop the repression, it will stop the depression.
It's time to protect our Earths soil.

Water making billboards, windmills and panels,
Using self created water as ignition source,
Create your own society, energy free
Keep the Earth safe, of course.

One True Friend (Part III)

I've known you now
For many years,
You helped me when
My eyes had tears.

You've been my friend
You've comforted me.
You helped me become
Who I'm supposed to be

You don't realise enough
Of what you have done.
You're one of my best friends
If not my best one.

A friend I hope
Will never leave.
If I were to lose you
I would surely grieve.

Pans

In the kitchen?
I don't know,
On top shelf?
Or below?

In the cupboard?
Maybe not,
Where are my pans?
I know not.

In the freezer
I don't think,
The cupboard under
The kitchen sink?

By the sugar?
It's not there
Where are my pans?
It's not fair.

Questions (Part I)

Now here's a question,
How is this all real?
Where did we come from?
Why do we feel?

How can we understand
The feelings we have now?
How do we know the answer
When all we ask is "how?"

So, what is the answer
To the questions we ask?
How do we realise
How to complete each task?

How do we pass through
Each and every day?
How do we find the right
Questions we want to say?

It's a weird old world,
It's a weird old place
It's a weird old journey
For a weird old race.

Solutions

So, what is my dream?
What is my passion?
Do I just copy others
In a parrot fashion?

I don't know what
Goes on upstairs,
I'm not sure
Who or what cares.

All I can do
To comfort myself
Is to keep writing
And seek real help.

So, will I improve
With a chemical inside?
Will it really help me
Not want to hide?

How do I control
My life like my cards?
Does it have anything to do
With my Astro-Chart?

Are dreams really the key
To releasing my mind?
Or is there another solution
That I will find?

Does keeping things in order
Reflect who I am?
Or is my mind full of rubbish?
Like a postman with spam.

Who Will?

It's hard to eat
When you're feeling down,
It's hard to stand
When you lose your crown.

It's hard to cope
When life throws things
Full force towards you,
Then angels lose their wings.

Who can hold you
When you want to crumble?
Who will be there
To prevent your stumble?

Who will do
What it takes to be there?
Who will prove
To you that they care?

Who will arrive
To help you succeed?
Who will be there
To get what you?

Who will hold out
Their hand like a glove?
Who will show emotion?
Who will show love?

One True Friend (Part IV)

Another person
That entered my life,
You will surely make someone
A beautiful wife.

You've known me since
The two thousandth year,
You've always helped me,
You've always been here.

Without you in my life
I would probably cry,
To be a friend to you,
I promise I'll try.

As I told you before,
I'm here until the end.
No matter what happens
You are my one true friend.

Holiday

Now this time
I will think
About where I am,
I'll check all
My emails,
I delete all my spam.

I check mail,
I flick through,
Then I choose one to read,
My brain absorbs
The information
My brain starts to feed.

I then get
My current account card
And type in the box,
I also get my camp hat,
My gloves and my suitcase.
I pack my new pair of socks.

I travel to the airport
I release worms
From a jar,
Then I get
On a plane
As I travel far.

I land in New York
For the release
Of my first book Footpath,
The New York
Book Exposition
Is where I unleashed my wrath.

The story has taken me
To saying some things
That I never thought I would say
About my thoughts of our home
Under our dome,
Living our life through each day.

Things are now different,
We can now see,
The differences in front of our eyes.
Spread the knowledge
That you have leaned
To take others by surprise!

Mighty Matt

This world is small
You travel it all
Yet you're still able to find
People you know
So you try to show
Them that you're loving and kind.

I wish I could explain
All about my pain,
I let my whole life slip,
All people say
Through every single day
Is "why don't you get a grip?"

They don't understand,
They hold up their hands
Nobody seems to care.
That is why
I lay and I cry
I feel like there's nobody there.

I still have words said
Into my head,
It's unusual, fancy that.
The person that talks
To me as I walk,
His name is Mighty Matt.

A Place

There's a place
In this world
That I would like to go,
A place that
If ever offered,
I could not say no.

There's a place
That I love
A place that feels like heaven
A place that's
In my mind,
It feels as pure as a reverend.

There's a place
That I think
I'd do anything to be there.
Now that place
Is my daydream,
It's becoming all so clear.

That place that I speak of
Is the other side.
The place you cannot see.
Though we'll be there,
And we've been there
It's where we'll always be.

Ignore the materiel,
Look at the nothing,
See the particles as they move.
Look for plasma shaped
Molecule-movements
And you'll know there's a different groove.

Force away the bad
Focus only on the pure
You know what's said is true.
Do not do what he tells you,
Do not sell it,
Because you know it belongs to you!

Money

For people who win
Jackpot amount,
When they have receipts everywhere,
More than they can count.

Money is worthless
In this silly old head
I'd rather be poor, but happy
Than sadly rich in my bed.

Money is Evil
Now, that I believe,
That's why I hate it
When money is received.

I don't like to have
More than my friends,
I will always share out
What I have until the end.

Money is nothing
But pain anger and grief,
So, a world without money
Would be perfect, I believe.

No Way

Brightness darkens,
The room's now dark.
All goes quiet,
Can't hear a dog's bark.

Walls close in,
I can hardly breathe,
Is this the trick that
The devil holds up his sleeve?

No place to escape,
No way to think.
Vision starts to spin
Like water down a sink.

Blackness takes over,
There's nowhere to hide.
I sit and I wonder,
When steel and flesh will collide.

Down and down
The spiral I spin.
No way to escape
No way to begin.

No way to run,
No way to get out.
No matter how much
I scream and I shout.

Darkness Brightens,
The room is now Bright
Watch those animals
Playing in the light.

What Do You Do?

What do you do when you feel unwell?
Do you take a pill?
What do you do when you're under a spell?
Do you write at your free will?

What do you do when you feel sad?
Do you take a drug?
What do you do when you act so badly?
Do you become a thug?

What do you do when you feel rage?
Do you punch the wall?
What do you do at that emotionless stage?
Do you crumble and do you fall?

What do you do when you are down?
Do you pray to above?
What do you do when you can't help but frown?
Do you look for love?

Some People (Part II)

Some people help,
Some people hurt,
Some praise your actions,
Others throw you in dirt.

Some people care,
Some people hate,
Some people don't believe,
Others believe in fate.

Some people are careless,
Some people are mean,
Some people are dirty,
Others try to be clean.

Some people are drunk,
Some people use drugs,
Some people are friendly,
Others try to be thugs.

Some people enjoy hurting,
Some people find it fun,
Some people have a path
That they have only just begun.

These people know the difference
Between what's right and what is wrong,
Some people know the answer
As to why they belong.

Those people spread the message
Of peace and truth and love,
Those people are like angels
Who fell from above

Cards of Life

It's hard to compare life
To a packet of cards,
But each one holds a story,
To explain it, it's hard.

The joker, the gesture,
The one that will smile,
Being held as a prisoner
For such a long while,

The kings of the packet,
The rulers of all,
With queens by their side
They always stand tall.

With the jacks to accompany,
With the suits they all face,
It's hard to explain,
The diabolical disgrace.

Fifty-two cards
Fifty-two weeks,
Four suits for four seasons
Each one's story will speak.

Something Tells Me

Something now tells me
That somebody will know,
Something of my mind
The information has shown.

Something now tells me
That the secret is out,
Something now tells me
That I must shout.

Something now tells me
That I cannot escape,
Something now tells me
That I've lost my cape

Something now tells me
That I'll be questioned by one,
Something now tells me
Complications have begun.

Something now tells me
That they know what's true,
Something now tells me
That they know what to do.

Something now tells me
That I will soon feel numb,
Something now tells me
That they don't think I'm dumb.

Realisation (Part I)

I've come to a realisation
That I know what I think,
It may have something to do
With the caffeine I drink.

I've come to a realisation
Those things in my head,
It may have something to do
With the way I sleep in my bed.

I've come to a realisation
That I'm not like another
It may have something to do
With the way I was raised by my mother.

I've come to a realisation
That I'm not quite the same,
It may have something to do
With the fact life feels like a game.

I've come to a realisation
Those things may be odd
But that's to do
With me being a silly old sod.

Jackie

This isn't a poem,
This isn't a lyric,
This is what I pray.
I never met you,
This is true,
But I think of her today

I wish her rest,
I wish her peace,
I wish her happiness above.
From what I heard,
She's loud and obscured
But she's full of love

She'll be missed by all
That's a fact
But she's no longer in pain,
So, I pray for her now
Even though I knew her not.
I look up at the sky through the rain.

A lady in heaven,
A lady of peace,
Shown in her own funny way,
Be restful, be peaceful,
We are all so grateful,
May all your problems go away.

Spice Girls

They told me what I wanted
What I really really wanted,
A super female pop group.
They sang out their hearts
But then they would part,
Dear lord, they jumped some hoops.

They went their own way
On an extraordinary day
There was Ginger and Scary Spice,
Victoria got married,
The rest got carried,
It wasn't very nice.

But then the amazing occurred,
It may sound obscured,
They re-united at last.
They began to tour
To entertain the poor,
They became a blast from the past.

From C to A

A dream that was real
The reality I feel
I stepped off the plane,
The first time in my life
I didn't need a knife,
I finally felt so sane.

I saw her face
I entered her place,
I held her close,
But a dream told me
Only then I could see
It was a temporary fantasy, of course.

I camped and I drove around
On a go-cart on the ground,
We want to watch a race,
I climbed a tree and looked
And I wrote some of a book,
I fell for her when I saw her face.

Then I got on a plane
And I got on a train
I went to New York City,
Even though that was fun,
I thought a new life had begun,
But I missed her, what a pity.

A day doesn't pass
When I don't think of the grass
That was then underneath my feet.
I keep asking my mind,
If it would be so kind
To never forget this memory-treat.

Comet-Line

Back to reality,
Back to routine.
Same old sh*t,
If you know what I mean?

Blooded Blue Blankets,
Washed each day.
Same old people
Repeated from June to May.

Can't help feeling: -
DeJaVu, each place,
Knowing you must escape
The evil life living place.

Everywhere I travel,
Who is to know?
Follow the stars, look past Mars.
The Comet-Line will glow.

Rich and Poor

I don't believe,
The world is right,
When we all rely on money.
The rich get fed,
The poor must starve,
Dear Lord, it isn't funny.

Advantage is taken,
By the people on top,
They rub it in our face.
Their time will come,
They'll feel the wrath,
They will know their place.

There's good and evil,
They battle each other,
But they battle through thicker and thinner.
They hide behind: -
Their camouflaged blinds,
And eat a four-course dinner.

While there's people here,
In this world,
Without a single pea.
So, do me a favour,
And help them out,
Let them drink some tea.

Verses

I always seem to start
With the word "I".
Well maybe the next verse
Will be different, let's try.

I guess I couldn't use
A different word.
Well maybe things will be different,
In verse the third.

I guess I just couldn't do it,
I just don't know the score,
Well I'll try a little harder
In verse number four.

I guess this verse
Is the same as the first three,
I guess this stupid poem
Is all about me.

You think that I am selfish?
You wish I weren't alive?
Well it's all about you
In verse number five.

Unsure

Unsure of where
I'm meant to be.
Unsure of whom
I'm meant to see.
Unsure of when
I make the right move,
Unsure of how
I dance to this groove.

Unsure of where
I'm meant to go to.
Unsure of whom
I'm meant to talk it through.
Unsure of why
I'm here on this earth,
Unsure of my destination
Of my death from my birth.

Unsure of the people: -
Who I should love and lust.
Unsure of the people
That I can trust.
Unsure of the location
That I'm supposed to live in,
Unsure of the life
That I want to begin.

Unsure of the food
That I'm meant to eat,
Unsure of the path
That I must walk with my feet.
I don't know what to do,
I don't know where to go,
I don't know who to speak to,
I don't know, I just don't know.

Scam

Mobile phones
And contracts,
They are all a scam.
They cause debt,
They cause pain,
They added to who I am.

They reel you in
Like a fish,
They trap you so fast.
They take your cash
From your pockets,
You wait to pay them off at last.

Their contracts
Are evil,
They hold you ransom.
They get all people.
They get ugly ones
And even the handsome.

So, you pay them,
And you follow
The path that they give.
Until you realise
That you've been scammed
And you feel like a div.

Arrange

You know in the bible
It says addiction is bad,
I'm fully addicted,
And no, I'm not glad.

I cannot escape
What keeps holding me back,
I feel like my head
Is under verbal attack.

Many moments to think about,
So much in my head,
Thoughts of the living,
Thoughts of the dead.

To arrange and to order
My thoughts every day,
It's like building a snowman
In the middle of May.

I wish you could hear
What they say to me,
Then you'd understand
That it's real, you see?

Will Not Go

I start to get
An achy feeling,
Down both sides of my head,
But no matter what I do,
It does not go
Even when I lie in my bed.

It grows through my skull,
The voice will start
And begin to talk to me,
So why don't it help,
When I try the
Relaxation therapy?

I must be honest,
When I relax,
The feeling will sometimes go,
But as soon as I tense,
My mind just cannot say no.

I get words thrown my way,
It circles my mind,
I feel like I will blow up,
So, what can I do?
Except ride it through
Whilst drinking Pepsi from my cup.

It's There

Some people come,
Some people go,
Some want to stay,
Some find it helps,
Some find it don't
Some people struggle through the day.

Some people don't know
What's wrong with their mind.
Some people know the truth.
Some people will hide,
Others will call
For help from the phone booth.

Some people fake it,
Some people will suffer,
Some people don't even care.
Real or not,
It won't be forgot,
Because I know it's there.

Judge

I maybe silent,
But my brain will shout,
I maybe smiling,
But my mind will pout.

I maybe laughing,
But my thoughts will scream.
I may be asleep
But I fear my dreams.

Hatred for nightmares,
How can I break free?
Voices and Visions
I hear them and see.

Friends and strangers,
Who can I trust?
Likeness and anger,
Love, Hate and Lust.

When I get angry,
I break some object,
I don't like to feel
Like I'm a reject.

I want acceptance,
I want to be known
For the person I am,
For the emotions I've show.

How can I be me?
When people around look?
Judging and criticizing me,
Whilst reading a book.

Bad Habits

One habit I have
Is biting my nails,
I chew them to the bone,
I do this all day.
While there's people around
And even when I'm alone.

Another habit is
Clicking my neck,
To help release tension,
I sometimes zone out
I enter a blank space.
Almost like a daydream dimension.

Something else that I do
That cannot be good,
I bite my bottom lip,
But I hide what I feel.
I keep thoughts to myself,
And drink Pepsi sip by sip.

One more bad habit,
That I need to fix,
Is not saying what's in my mind,
But I do not want
People to know
The truth that keeps us blind.

Just Like

Just like ash,
From a cancer stick.
Just like flowers
From a magic trick.

Just like words,
From a beautiful song.
Just like the devil,
Always doing wrong,

Just like the birds,
That sings from the tree,
Just like the buzzing
From a bumble bee.

Just like a sound
That an animal will make,
Just like the scraping sound.
Of a garden rake.

Just like happiness,
Your smile will increase.
Just like the monkeys,
You will climb the trees.

Just like an idiot.
Dressed like a clown.
Just like emotions,
They go up down.

Begin

Everybody's different
Each person who cares.
All different coloured eyes,
All different coloured hair.

All different minds,
To process each brain,
Different thoughts to
Keep us all sane.

So, what must we all do?
Is what we want to know.
How do we feel love,
That we all want to show?

How do we know what
We must do today?
How do we find out
The games we all play?

I wish I could come to
A conclusion on things.
But where does it all start?
Where does it begin?

Pointers

When times get hard,
Take a step back.
When life is scary,
When you feel like you've lost track,

When you start to worry,
That you won't get better,
When your mind is funny,
Write a friend a letter.

When you don't know
Quite what to do,
When you cannot show
What you've been through.

I know that things
Will always work out.
The birds will sing,
There's no need to shout.

Empty your mind.
Clear your head,
Always be kind,
Share your bread.

When you panic
That you won't improve,
Stay positive when sick,
You'll find a whole new groove.

Some People (Part III)

Some people listen,
Some people don't,
Some people help,
Some people won't.

Some people stand,
Some people sit,
Some people do a lot,
Some only does a bit.

Some people are good,
Some people are bad,
Some people lose a lot
Of what they had.

What left is there then?
The time will be when?
It will come sooner or later,
Prove yourself that you're greater.

Kill the demon inside,
No need to hide,
Just evacuate and toss it away.
The goodness you want,
The mighty happiness taunt,
The angel you want to stay.

Do well, be nice,
Love what you want to do.
Be loving your every action,
Do the things that make you true.

Real Love

Like a beam of sunshine,
Like a breath of fresh air.
Like a smell of a flower,
Like a card game that's fair.

Like a glimpse of heaven,
With gold pearly gates,
Like a peaceful churchyard,
No evil, no hate.

Like a good cup of Deaf,
Like a hug from a friend.
Like a soft pillow fight,
No need to defend.

Like a feeling of goodness,
Is how you make me feel,
Like a rose from a garden,
Please know my love's real.

Different Direction

Playing with fire,
Fighting with flames.
Not knowing cheat codes,
To complete these life games.

Jumping through hoops,
Like a circus act.
But an act is not like this,
Now that is a fact.

How do I stabilize?
My life from now on?
Because it now feels like,
It has all gone wrong.

So, what can I do now
To rectify my mistakes?
I don't know the answers,
I ask for goodness sake.

So, I lay on my bed,
And talk to the wall,
Wondering if I'm sane,
Or crazy after all.

What's for You?

If you're common,
Have coffee.
If you're rich,
Have some tea.

If you're young,
Have some Cola,
If you're Kel,
Have orange soda.

If you're me,
Have Pepsi,
If you're fat,
Have Diet, you brat.

Military Defence

I must say
On this day
That someone is strange.
I'm unsure
If this guy
Is sane or deranged.

He rambles,
He goes on
About weird things.
He's confused
In his mind
But he knows where to begin.

He talks about
The army, Roswell
And military Defence,
He then gave me some money
Two pound and sixty pence.

He believes
Such strange things
He thinks it's all true.
He's comical,
He's serious,
He's nuts through and through.

Ghosts (Part I)

Some people can see them,
Some people cannot.
Some people ignore them,
Some people see a lot.

Some people can't help it,
It shows in their face,
Some people zone out
And stare into space.

Some people don't believe
That they exist,
Some people get frustrated,
So, they use their fist.

Some people will lose it
Some would drop their Sunday roast.
Some people get frightened,
When they see a ghost.

Some people walk through them
By accident.
It happened in darkness,
But the goosebumps went.

Stay calm, just know,
They cannot hurt you,
They may try to take a part,
But remember what's true.

Pressure

Pressure by government
To follow their rules,
But they don't understand everyone,
They don't have the tools.

They criticize each person,
They judge and they force: -
Good people into poverty,
They think they're in charge of course.

But they cannot keep going
The way they are.
They keep pushing each person,
To walk away so far.

They must realise that each,
Person is different on earth.
Not all people are leaders,
That was established at birth.

Some people are scared,
This is so true.
Some people just don't know
What to do.

Devil

The time has come,
I look to the floor,
The devil watches below.
The anger he throws,
The violence he shows,
The hatred will grow.

He tempts you, he tries you,
He tests your mind,
To see if you will listen.
He takes each measure,
He hides a treasure,
His anger shines and glistens.

He hides evil around us,
He controls his puppets,
He cares not for you.
So, don't sell your soul,
Just live your sole role,
His anger is so true.

There's only one follower
In this universe,
That we all need to know.
God is his name,
He is true fame,
He created our life which isn't slow.

Never

Hair of beauty
Brown and long,
A feeling came to me.
I failed my duty,
I lost that song,
It wasn't meant to be.

A love that I felt,
I thought she felt alike,
Then she stabbed me in the back.
But love is an element,
Unlike any other,
You cannot stick it with blue tack.

Once parted, once finished,
The feeling will go,
It cannot be repaired.
Feeling and emotions,
Just like your visions,
They can become Impaired.

I wish I could tell you
How I felt,
When I thought her love was true,
But suddenly,
She decided to leave me
And left me in the blue.

It's an awesome feeling,
That love I felt,
But it's gone now and forever.
But no matter how hard I try,
But no matter how much I cry,
We will never be together.

Full of It

Find a deer,
The glass is clear.
If you drink,
Do not steer.

Take in a sheep,
The hill is steep.
Lay there quietly
If you cannot sleep.

Don't be a doorknob,
Get a job,
I care not one bit,
You're full of it.

Place on Earth

Is there a place on Earth that can be found:-
That is different to how we live?
Is there a human alive on the ground: -
That has feelings they cannot give?

Is there an eternal place that holds the key: -
To peace and love on Earth?
Is there a Mother and Father who knows the world differently: -
To teach their kids from birth?

Is there a place to go to be yourself: -
Is there a place where you can hide?
Is there a playground in Heaven and a roundabout in Limbo?
And to get to Hell on a slide.

If you had the chance to start again: -
Would you say yes?
If you got asked the question which direction?
Would you hazard a guess?

Life's Puzzles

Yellow sunshine, Clouds are grey,
Rain will fall throughout the day.
Just like tears, they get in our way,
Unable to enjoy, unable to play.

A puzzle book life is what this is,
Temper's like Pepsi, ready to fizz.
Life's questions get asked, like a long pub quiz,
It's like a public test involved in our biz.

We try to find where we're meant to go,
Temptations around, it's hard to say no.
It feels like a punch, we fall to the floor.
Just when we get somewhere, we find a locked door.

Flip a coin, deal the cards, it's time to take a chance.
Each chance we take, each little mistake, we find no romance.
Look around, look for truth, go on, and just take a glance.
Wait for the day, what can I say? I want to sing and dance.

Hold the paper and the pen and write down what you feel,
Mix your potions, hide your emotions, it helps you to feel free.
Hold in your tears, hide your fears,
That's what it's like to be me.

Zau 7

It states in The Bible
Both Adam and Eve
Didn't realise they were naked,
Until the apple they received.

They took a bite because
The serpent persuaded them to.
They know the difference between,
Good and evil, lies and what's true.

Weather that story's real,
Or if it's a metaphor,
That I don't know,
The answer is behind a closed door.

One thing I know,
The story explains
Be good, do right,
And heaven remains.

There's no evidence or proof,
To say that it's true,
But you can decide for yourself,
If God's heaven is for you.

U-Turn (Part 1)

He's sitting there, idle and still
Wondering how to get his thrill.

Where must he go?
He does not know,
He thinks and gets flustered.
His thoughts are immense,
They make no sense,
Like ice cream with mustard.

It may seem
Like his life is a dream,
Characters float away.
His way of pulling through
And learning what to do,
Is remembering his sights each day.

But when can he learn
To make a U-Turn?
And focus his visualisations,
Put actions to words,
It may sound obscured,
He knows there's a destination.

He takes a bath,
He plans a path,
The turning he must take,
It's almost inter-dimensional
He packs his essentials
His alarm clock will awake.

Third Time Lucky

The strange thing is that I
Have done this before
Like DeJaVu
I get my pen from the drawer.

I typed it, I stored it,
Then I lost it all,
I kicked myself and cursed,
I felt all so small.

I done it the second time,
And it vanished to my mistake.
I thought that I'd give up,
It gave me heartache.

This third time I'll do it
With paper and a pen
So, I know that I won't
Lose it again.

I'll store it, I'll keep it,
In a super safe place.
If I lose it again,
It'll be a disgrace.

Starting New (Part II)

Sitting still, not much fun.
Almost encouraging to get up and run.
Hide from people I don't want to see,
Start life new and just be free.
I did it once, I packed a bag
I got up, lit a cigarette and took a drag,
Then I started to stroll, started to walk,
I listened to the voices that always talk.
I look for signs, I pray to the sky,
I asked for comfort for what I try.
I travelled the whole of the UK, it still wasn't right,
No matter how hard I tried, I couldn't sleep at night

It's one thing to leave your past behind,
To look for a new place, and new friends to find.
To start again, it's an exciting thing,
To have a new life to start and begin.
But after a while, you start to think
About your past and times when you used to drink,
You'll miss all your friends, your family too
You start to wonder how it's possible to pull through.

Yes, it's easy to start again on your own
But that's just it, you're all alone.
Nobody around you to comfort and hold,
You see how your life begins to unfold.
So, just start a new page,
Think of your life,
Try not to think
Of finding a wife.
Be yourself, don't judge,
You do not have the right,
Enjoy your moments, do what you must,
Get used to things that fill you with fright.

There's good, there's bad
In this world around,
Collect sentimental items
From places you've found.

Just jump into life's ride,
Yes, it's hard not to hide.
When it all boils down,
It's time to mention money,
Even though it might
Not even seem that funny.

Money is an evil element
Created to control
Unfortunately for us,
It's taken over us all.

Success

Erase bad ideas,
Pay off old arrears,
Get yourself out of this hole.
Digging yourself deeper,
It gets all so steeper.
Do you believe you're a mole?

Use the tools you have,
Use what you can
To complete your destination,
Be the good person
That you are,
Do not show your frustrations.

Honesty, Truthful,
Decent being
Is what you want to be.
Continue that road
Spreading the knowledge,
Help others to be free.

Look miles away,
One lighthouse to another,
See the truth within.
Ask the questions,
Find your answers
About the plane that we live in.

If you think
That I'm joking,
Look at my face,
Lies exposed,
Truth is open,
Look at the place.

Little Mix

Do you want to know
A weird little mix?
Well here's what I do
To get my little fix.

It is not a drug
It is not a drink
It cannot be bad
Well, at least I don't think.

It may sound weird,
It may sound strange,
It may sound a little different,
It has a various range,

Do you want to know
What is this little scoop?
It's Princes Hot Dog Sausages
With Chicken and Mushroom Soup.

I See

I see cuts,
I see blood,
I see someone
In the mud.

I see pain,
I see tears,
I see death,
I see fear.

I see hurt,
I see grief,
I see people
In disbelief.

I see sadness,
I see confusion,
I see anger
In this living illusion.

I see family,
I see friends,
I see these images
Coming to an end.

I see love,
Through a scope.
I see peace,
I see hope.

Time (Part I)

You listen to silence,
You hear a tick, tock.
You look up at the time
That's on the face of the clock,

Time is unusual,
But it's so accurate to date,
It tells you if it's day or night,
It shows you your fate.

If you don't understand the concept
Of a clock like I do,
Take a second to think,
How time had come through.

It started with the sun
Starting with day and night.
When the clouds blow over so much,
When the stars are shining bright.

But time can hide
All sorts of things,
Like it holds an everlasting emotion,
Like an angel without wings.

But the one thing about time
That seems to cause confusion,
Is that time itself
Is just one big illusion.

Time isn't real,
You sleep when you need,
It's the same as hunger,
That's when you feed.

Living in the moment,
You now here,
Spend your time in love
And don't waste it in fear.

Dear

If you're aware of the shadows,
Keep your awareness in the light.
Look up far to the stars
As you pray at night.

Ignore that dark shadow
As you climb the mountains.
Be prepared for your journey
Drink from the water fountains.

With immortality, walk through fire,
Beware the armadillo's wrath,
Just one bite from him at night
You'll have troubles in your path.

Keep on walking this adventure,
It is your destiny.
Love your family, love your friends,
Spread truth in unity.

Spread the peace, tell no lies,
Speak directly from the heart.
Walk the garden to see the horizon
Even though you're miles apart.

Nature generates disturbing beauty,
Please do not feel grief,
I forever am here beside you
To hold a handkerchief.

The beer in bars that we all see
Can hurt you deep inside.
Genuinely transcend your deep emotions,
I swear you won't need to hide.

Compose your fate; it's not too late,
Continue forever your enlightenment.
Your eventual success will be the best,
Your light inside honestly never went.

As quintessential as you are,
You like to have your fun.
Use generosity in your direction,
And know I love you, son.

Differentiate

When I sit here
I can't help but scribble down.
When my hands shake,
I can't help but frown.

When I get lost
In my little old world,
When I daydream
About life and about girls.

When I can't tell
What is real or not,
What can I do
Except scribble and jot?

What is the way
To where must I skate?
How do I find my way?
How do I find my fate?

Surrounding Environment

Whilst sitting on the toilet
The idea came forth.
I listened to music
As I travelled north.

I passed a purple tree,
And pulled out my papers.
Green cannabis inserted, mind re-diverted,
I light the spark for different flavours.

I keep my soul in the light,
As I travel in the night.
To protect myself with all might,
To counteract freight.

Force fed emotional pain
To enslave us running through my mind.
But I keep myself conscious
To stop myself from being blind

I keep my chakra in a bubble
I keep my eyes open wide,
The tyrant who once ruled before
Is not
The one who will hide.

A spark of energy from a magazine,
Helping the dreamers to keep dreaming.
Whilst the ones who are awake sparked and
Are stood behind them screaming.

Meditation will help them
Alleviate the pain in the heart.
The ghost in the darkness
Will be kept far apart.

I walk over a tump of compost
And I climb over a locked gate,
I travel the mountains,
It is my fate.

I see the slaves procrastinate,
They walk whilst in a dream,
Whilst watching a midget on their device,
It makes me want to scream.

They inject themselves with sadness
It leaves a sting, it must be said.
Whilst trapping themselves in a harness,
With a gold ring under their bed.

The thoughts of death would smudge their brain,
They hear of an elephant on a boat.
The wind then blows a pleasant breeze
Almost like it hit a special note.

Blues comes on my headphones,
Before peanut butter jelly
I reach the end of my smoke,
I admit it was rather smelly,

I see a police house, I eat an apple,
A policeman has a ride in style,
Lower gears to erase their fears
I just walked a mile.

In my backpack, a rope for climbing,
To climb a mountain with ease.
I keep my chakras in a happy state,
I enjoy a pleasant breeze.

I reach the peaks, at a pinpoint,
Below now, seems so small.
I glide below. Well, what do you know?
There's now old in my palm.

I stack some wood and catch a chicken,
I pray for eternity.
I eat a lemon and think of heaven,
I head back to the city.

I see a hole, I jump, and I land,
I continue in my path.
I buy a rubber duck as a souvenir
To enjoy while I'm in the bath.

Helping

It's surprising
How many get involved
It's interesting to watch
Humanity evolves.

It's crazy to experience
All different types
Whilst cleansing our souls
With baby wipes.

We can work together
And help this earth
We can help humanity
Starting from birth

All this commotion
All our support
The time has come
To no longer fort.

We all do our part
By helping people all around
By travelling each path
With both feet on the ground.

By working together
We can all get by,
Whilst having some fun.
We can make our time fly.

Everything we do,
Will eventually work out
By using teamwork,
That's what it's all about.

Exhibitor

So, we're on day two,
Again, it has begun,
We all gather together,
We start to have some fun.

Superheros and Villains,
They are all around.
No matter where we are
They are all making a sound.

We all work together
In creating an atmosphere
Some are drinking water
And some are drinking beer.

Stalls and shops
All selling their assets
Travelling from countries
All placing their bets.

The exhibition in all
Are all very nice,
If you think they are not,
You'd better think twice.

All the fun that happens
In the arena,
Then I stumble and slip
Into a cleaner.

Thoughts Can Be Similar

All I need for a favour,
Is a piece of paper?
And either a black or blue pen?
And I will write
Throughout the night,
My thoughts from now and then.

Each thought can be similar,
But others can differ,
But they have the same message,
So, when I talk to myself.
About needing help.
I look for a knife by the fridge.

So, what makes me feel
Like I don't know what's real,
I lose my short-term memory,
So, to help me remember,
I've become a member,
Of a group called "Insanity"

I may one day
Realise what I say,
And take my own advice,
But for goodness sake.
I want the whole cake,
Not just one darn slice.

Accident Prone

You wake up
And bump your head on the wall,
Well it's not that hard
When your six-foot tall.

You stand up,
Feeling all groggy,
Then you fall down the stairs
By tripping over your doggy.

You get up
And get your PG Tips,
But you drink it too quickly
And burn your lips.

You quickly drink water,
But it sniffs up your nose,
You start to sneeze,
Water and tea drips on your toes.

You decide to listen
To your favourite band
But you drop the CD player
And it breaks your hand.

You rush to get
To A & E
Then you stand on your glasses
And you're unable to see.

You walk around
Like Mr. Magoo.
And you walk into the door
Instead of walking through.

You then go to the opticians
And walk through the door.
You shout "I Need some glasses please"
You then hear "You certainly do, this is a record store!"

The First Stepping Stone of Movement

Years will pass, can't look back.
Getting up to music: -
Rap Metal Black.
Same old clothes,
Same old large Sack.
A different outcome, a whole new start.
A new way to focus, a new way to set a heart.
Following breadcrumbs like Hansel and Gretel,
Wondering of that location to finally kick back and settle.

Following signs, finding conclusions,
Learning what to believe
And what are just illusions.
Dreams with an impact,
Showing the Possibility.
Whilst hiding behind this black cloak
Of endless everlasting invisibility.

Time to break, for goodness sake.
Time for this body alarm clock to awake.
A whole new brand, a whole new make.
A place to escape and never be fake.
The memories of the life, grown behind four walls,
Through the ups and downs,
Through the rise and falls.
A place that created this hidden soul.
But things change, we move on to the next role.

A role in life that explains what's true.
A role in life that determines what to do.
Reaching the junction.
Which way is wrong or right?
Will these dreams give the answer?
With each sleep at night?
These prays and pleads towards life and humanity,
Wondering and concerned about true insanity.
Pains and distractions,
What's the reaction?
Fifty-fifty Heads or Tails,
By gosh, what a fraction.

Time (Part II)

Time of life
Passes each day
Think about the minutes
That we've thrown away.

Think of the time that we've wasted,
As we age every night,
Think of the time we have spent
In fear and in fright.

Think of how we waste
Our time doing nothing
And how we wished we spent our time
Doing at least something.

Think about the dreams
We always wanted to do,
Think of the people we met
Along the way, too.

Think about your life,
Don't waste another dime,
Be creative, live for real,
Life's short, don't waste your time.

The Reason

A reason to take,
A reason to give,
A reason to die,
A reason to live.

There's a reason
In the back of your mind,
A reason why you sometimes
Try to be kind.

There's a reason
Why you try to be nice,
A reason you take chances
Whilst rolling a dice.

There's a reason
For all that's in life,
A reason that a couple
Becomes husband and wife.

There's a reason
Why you look up above,
And that reason is
You want to feel love.

A reason to help,
A reason to see,
A reason to exist,
A reason to be.

Tŷ Gwyn

There's a place on this planet
Of which I know…
A place that took me in
When I had nowhere to go.
A place that has fed me
Practically every day
A place that has helped me
To find my way.

There's a place on this planet
That uses Christmas lights
A place that makes sure
I'm home every night
A place that ensures
Safety comes first.
Its beauty may not be as impeccable as Canada
But it sure as hell isn't the worst.

There's a place on this planet
That seems to have accepted me,
A place that has helped me
Get to where I must be.
A place that ensures
That nothing goes wrong,
A place where it's ok
To feel like you belong.

There's a place on this planet,
There's a place on this earth.
Destiny has brought me here,
It's been awaiting my birth.
There's a place that I can compliment,
But where do I begin?
This amazing homely place,
It's called Tŷ Gwyn.

Time (Part III)

Time of rest,
Time of peace,
Time running out,
Time being increased.

Time to walk,
Time to run,
Time for fun
Has begun.

Time to write,
Time to rhyme,
Time to play,
Time to climb.

Time to finish
What I have to say,
Time to scream
"Have A Nice Day!"

All Around

Look at the universe, look to the stars,
Wonder who you are and where to travel far.
Wonder what's the meaning of why we're truly here?
But the answer to the question is what we all fear.

I sometimes feel like life doesn't exist,
That's why I cut myself, to feel something on my wrist.
Vision is like a videogame in 3D HD,
Sometimes I worry about what I might see.

For that reason, above, I'd like to awake,
I try to please others and not make a mistake.
I follow rules and I try to impress humans all around,
I hold the world, bottle it up then crumble to the ground.

People tell me "things get better", they tell me "cheer up".
But I can't help my tears falling slowly in my cup.
They say I got OCD. I put everything in its rightful place.
Sometimes I feel if life was a person, I'd hit it in the face.

My family drifted, my friends apart, I know not what to do,
I just live this life, I hold the knife, and yet I still try and pull through.
"How can I live a life in sorrow?" I ask myself each day,
I burst out with anger, I feel so hollow, what more can I say?

Where's My Head?

One night I went to bed,
Asking "where's my head?"

I found my head under the bed
Eating a loaf of bread

The next day I got out of the bed
Shouting "I found my head"

My mother said, "Where was your head?"
I said, "It was under my bed."

Comicon 2016

Cardiff is the location,
It's where we are.
On our back-door step
We didn't travel far.

Out of the property
Onto the train
Out to the coldness,
Out to the rain.

No matter the location,
No matter where we go,
The destination that waits
Shall always await us so.

We try to be truthful,
We do what we can,
We follow our actions,
We follow our plan.

We stick to our footsteps,
We stick to our path,
We learn our literature,
We practice our math.

Stepping Forward (Part I)

When you're sitting in pain
With a mind overload.
And you feel like it's time
To jump overboard.

When you want to see blood
Drip from your skin,
When the anger and rage
Takeover begins.

When you're feeling so little,
Feeling so small,
When you feel like driving
Your fist through a wall.

When you lose track of your mind,
And not know what to do,
When you've had enough
And feel like you're through.

When you feel like screaming
And you can't take anymore,
Just stand up and take
A step through the door.

Go for a walk,
Go to the trees,
Admire the nature,
Whilst on your knees.

Pray to the lord,
Look to the sky,
Ask for your answers,
Or at least, try.

Ghosts (Part II)

Do you believe in ghosts?
Because this, yes, I do.
I've seen shadows moving,
As well as objects, they're trying to get though.

They try to talk to people who listen: -
But they cannot communicate.
Unless you find you place your mind: -
In that unconscious state.

If you listen hard and squint your eyes,
You never know, you might see them there.
But don't force yourself and don't force them,
Because we all know that isn't fair.

Relax your eyes, look around,
You'll see the hidden movement.
You will know the truth and see what's real,
And know the time they spent.

Time (Part IV)

It's about that time.
We just woke up.
The kettle is on
To fill our cup.

It's about that time
We log on and share
Relevant information
To show that we care.

It's about that time
That we block out the lies,
Keep sharing the truth,
Let old ways be goodbyes.

It's about that time,
That we made a call
To prevent future issues
Becoming the reasons that we fall.

It's about that time
Where we get together
Focus our brains
To maintain forever.

It's about that time
That we should all see
That in due time
What will be will be.

Conquer

To join the fun,
To join the craze,
To walk around
In a daze.

To learn the truth
To know what to do.
To jump in the deep end.
To know what is true.

To walk the mile
To keep walking forward.
To remain positive
Without feeling awkward.

To skip the steps
That matters the least,
To focus on importance
And conquer the beast.

To jump in a fire
With water to put out.
To land in there barefoot
With no need to shout.

To stick to what
You know is right.
To know that nightmares,
Keeps you awake at night.

To conquer the problem,
To remain on top
To clean up all issues
By using a mop.

Old Friends

It's always nice
To visit an old friend,
It's always nice
When friendships don't end.

It's always nice
To see somewhere new,
Whether you travel by train
Or whether you got on a plane and flew.

It's always nice
To help when you can.
It's always nice
To see a random tram.

It's always nice
When your friends smile,
Especially when you haven't
Seen them for a while.

A catch-up is sweet
Even when you've only met twice,
So, dance to the beat
Because it's always nice.

What Do We Really Know?

"We're on a ball".
Say's the CGI.
Do these cartoons
Tell us a lie?
Toy spinner in the corner,
Memories implanted,
Do we take the subliminal
Signals for granted?

Water sticks
To a spinning ball.
Apparently, gravity is the reason
Those things will fall.
However, we must remember
That it's only a theory.
The spinning has never
Made me feel weary.

"We revolve around
A great ball of fire"
Is what they say,
But it's not true desire.
Not thirty, but: -
Ninety-three million miles away
Is the scientific fact,
According to what they say.

Sideways Satellites,
Tall wired towers,
Pointing in the same direction
During all of hours.
Was it the International Space station?
Or a U2 spy plane?
Please don't let their lies
Drive you insane.

Boats over curvature,
You think it's gone?
Nikon P900 Zoom,
It's been there all along.
Lighthouses apart,
Thousands of miles across the sea,
We can see that curvature
Simply cannot be.

The Van Allen we cannot pass
Because it was "discovered"?
Well, it debunks the moon landings,
Their lies have been uncovered.

Media Outlets,
What propaganda sings,
Sharing the lie
Whilst they know what the truth brings.
A handful of puppets, a handful of rebels,
Each side knows what's true.
Whilst the masses awaken to the true beginning,
Each handful will know what to do.

True tech awareness awakens,
The times have now started,
Those lives that we lived in the past,
Those different memories have now been parted.
"Another place, another time."
Is what many people say
Work together, spread peace forever,
Spread love to battle this day.

Remember the times, remember the dreams,
Remember what you're meant to do.
Know your meaning, know your purpose,
You know you'll see this through.
The sun may circle, the moon also,
The earth may stand still,
But know there's a reason; know there's an answer,
And you will remember true will.

To Live

To list achievements that I've achieved,
To list beliefs that I believe,
To list the doings that I have done,
To walk this footpath that I've begun.

To walk through rain at night in the cold,
To think about life and growing old,
To know the past and what's happened so far,
To open a can, like worms in a Jar.

To get trophies and certificates for martial arts,
To get hurt by loved ones and get broken hearts,
To receive advice from people above
To look for answers, to look for love.

To meet people in life, both evil and good,
To know what a sin is and to do what you should,
To run with the wind and try to be free,
To not know what to do, that's what it's like to be me.

To examine each footstep, to run away far,
To refuse to use petrol or drive in a car,
To refuse the technology that's placed in my hand
To learn to snap back like a rubber band.

To know what to do is an impossible game,
To live a life of sadness is a real shame,
To know who your friends are and to show them love,
To continue asking questions to God that's above.

So Many

So many people,
So many locations,
So many societies
In so many nations.

So many troubles,
So many fears,
So many prayers
That the sky one day clears.

So many questions
So many riddles
So many corporations
Like Walmart and Lidl.

So many politicians
So many speakers
So many people
Run far in their sneakers.

So many issues,
But let's be bold.
How much help
Do we all hold?

Destination

Different beliefs
That we all feel,
A jumble of information
Can we work out what's real?
All different feelings,
All different gods,
From all different religions
Stored on people's iPods.

We must put the pieces together
And decide for ourselves
While re reach to see what help
Is placed on the shelves.
Take in all the information
And you can decide
Whether you want to be free,
Or whether you want to hide.

We gather our knowledge
We know what is true,
We determine our answers.
You'll continue to pull through
In the end, we all realise,
No matter where you are
You can get where you want,
No matter how close or far.

All that matters in the end
As we conclude our destination,
Is that we must be kind,
As we are having our fun.

Show

So, this is
Now the end
Of this bizarre old book,
If you can relate
To what I've said,
Take another look.

The truth is out there,
I promise you that
One day someone will find,
They will share it
With us all,
They will free our mind.

I apologise
That I can't answer
This life's riddle,
So, ask someone else
Maybe a musician
Or somebody with a fiddle.

But if I discover
One day or another
What we want to know,
I'll share it with you,
I promise that's true
I'll perform for you, a show.

From now until next time,
I bid thee farewell.
I pray that you may find
That "Poems of Positivity"
Can eliminate Negativity.
It can help you ease your mind.

Poem of Positivity (Part I)

Focus your mind, try to stay kind
Please don't be blind,
Slide through life like grease,
But always share peace.

You may travel far,
By plane or by car,
But we're all the same,
It's our shared-life game.

Let's play fair with each and all,
Referee your life when you play ball,
And if life seems like it's bouncing off a wall
Just shrug it off and smile and stand tall.

Have fun on our earth
From our moment of birth,
Some of you don't realise
How much you're all worth.

Forget the old mirror, look within.
Find peace, no matter where you start.
I wonder what you'll find,
Just stay true with your heart.

Part II

Chapter 1

Walking Through Heavy Traffic

Introduction

My name is Tommy, there's a voice called Steven, fancy that...
This is a story that is just a beginning
We've been through a lot, but we'll get to that.
I've seen the stories of hell, that taste of bugs and the nasty smell.
For a reason that's obvious, my soul I won't sell.
Take a glance at this random mix
These tales and stories will be told.
You can see the truth, it begins to unfold.
Now then, you entities of love,
You decide for yourself what's true.
The invitation's extended,
Way beyond me and you
A past life has now been acknowledged,
The truth is dished up on a tray
Now, here we go again...
...HAVE A NICE DAY!!

Realities (Part I)

Plans that were made,
Memories will fade,
It's a restoration of a thought plan.
What do we see?
How do we learn who we're meant to be?
And where do we find "the man"?

Realities collide,
There's nothing to hide,
The particles are smashing together.
Electrons and neutrons,
Protons and Photons
Our reality has changed forever.

The Kit-Kat hyphen has gone,
It now feels so wrong,
Memories have disappeared.
Logos in a book,
No matter where we look,
Things have changed, I fear.

Technological advances,
Taking second glances,
These changes, are we sure?
Avoiding the death,
Avoid Satan's breath.
Try your best to be pure.

Repent your sins,
You will begin
To see what is true,
The globe has gone,
NASA is wrong,
Work together is what we must do.

Some was spent,
Some was made,
Lessons learned,
Memories fade.

Some come back
They throw us off track
But we remember to stay strong.
We will learn,
We will turn,
We will beat to our favourite song.

We do know,
Those feelings so.
We see them within our eyes.
We feel what's true
With all that we do.
Believe me, there's no surprise.

Breakdown Recovery

You think I moved from one location
To just get away from a fool,
I moved from that location
To be closer to someone cool.

Half way closer,
Living in a bar,
But still not close enough,
I still live too far.

A little bit closer,
In a caravan,
Not enough space though
For our little man.

Make myself homeless and
Live in a b&b for the holidays
Hoping that I'll have a place
For my family to play.

In a nice big flat,
For the space, I am glad.
Still not live together,
My son doesn't live with his dad.

Another place on the horizon,
Plenty of rooms to play,
Won't live with me though,
Since the start I have moved more than half way.

No matter my location,
the answer is a no.
I'm starting to feel like
You will not let go.

I am feeling like
I have to move all the way.
No say in anything, school, home
Nothing. No meeting half way.

I feel like no matter what I do
And no matter where I go,
Nothing is good enough
Nothing I do no more.

I am on the verge
Of breaking down;
I try to fake a smile
To hide my blatant frown.

I sacrificed my life once
For somebody else in the past.
Even though I was rejected,
Even though it didn't last.

I guess I just feel like
I am going around the bend
And I guess I just feel like
I'm going through it all over again,

The light at the end
Has now proved to me,
That without this person,
I would not now be free.

We have let go,
We are no more,
Now where will I score
As I walk on the floor?

Run

It's so easy to just
Pack a bag and leave,
Nobody would miss me,
Nobody would grieve.

I could start a life
That is brand new,
I could find a love,
That I know is true.

I could get these thoughts
Out of my head,
I could escape the feelings
Of wanting to be dead.

I could run and run
Forever and ever,
I could find a soul-mate
And live happily together.

I could run,
I could hide,
Just waiting for thousands
Of realities to collide

I could run,
I could be free,
I could be hide secrets,
But that's not me

I could start a new life
And then another one
I could start to run
But that's not fun.

I could run,
But I'd rather walk
And absorb the emotions
Of which is thought

I could look up
To that darkened old sun
Hiding from truth,
I could just run.

I could be honest,
I could be true,
Running isn't what
I really want to do.

Reunited

I met my brother
Finally, at last
Since his existence was established,
So much time has passed.

He's my brother,
He is here.
He's a good guy,
This I'm sure.

A random twist
To life's little mix,
A different experience
With nothing to fix.

Look at shooting stars,
Impaired vision? Use a telescope.
My wish upon that star came true.
I found my brother, a friend, I hope.

Keep in contact,
Keep in touch
Because this family relationship
Has meant so much.

Things in common
I can't explain,
He drove me home
To keep me dry from rain.

Twenty-five years apart,
Reunited tonight.
Family importance
Is in my sight.

Honour and cherish
Those close to you.
Because one thing for sure,
Is families love being true.

A Random Journey

After eating salmon
On a cloudy day,
I listened to music
Along the way

Whilst on the beach
Listening to the ocean waves,
A jeep drove up
And it passed the caves.

Inside this jeep,
There was a cat and a dog,
They were attached to a trailer
This contained an Owl and a Frog

A humble man stood.
As he stood wide awake,
His friends walked by
With a prize to take.

He held a piece of an onion,
He felt happy and complete.
Even though he knew
He had gout on his feet.

But the collective combination decided
Together they would stand,
Because the truth that lays behind
They could truly understand.

Individually they collected
Their portfolio for their family
Individual travels to locations away,
Whilst tuned into the conscious connecting tree.

A mouth touched the microphone
As he began to speak,
Towards the crowd he looked,
Then his speech reached his peak.

Family and friends would gather
To create their custom flow.
Sometimes towards the water,
And on the ships will go.

Underneath there was a whale,
With his talents, he's guided the way.
Then the sun broke through the clouds
And light shone across the way.

On an island, there's a hostel,
With a simple harmonica to celebrate,
There are random locations for healing
Whilst escaping locations of hate.

Then a helicopter picked them up
And flew them all to Sweden's centre,
In the chopper, posters of charts
Prepped them for an adventure.

Yet they could not abandon
The fitting glove from the past,
It was yellow in colour,
But it was ambient, at last.

Stepping Forward (Part II)

I hear the voices, I follow
I live my life, so hollow
I live a life with sorrow,
Happiness I wish I could borrow.

I wake up in the morning,
Or more like the afternoon,
I look around for love.
A love that was lost so soon.

I care for each person,
I try to show all love
But it's hard to feel emotions
Whilst you're praying to above

It's hard to do the right thing,
When it's impossible to do,
But when you got a hand to hold,
You know you will pull through.

For those who has no hand,
To hold throughout the night.
Just know that you can survive,
You know that you must fight.

Maybe not with violence,
Not with anger, but with emotion,
Just follow your life through,
Live through each day, throughout commotions.

Pass the test, Get an "A"
Do the best you can
Live your, try your best,
You are not superman.

If you feel like you've failed,
Take a step and think about who you are,
Start again, take one step more,
Begin to walk quite far.

One True Love

It's been a long time
Since I fell into the hands: -
Of a princess to me.
I miss the blood pumping through my glands.

I'd love to have someone
To hug and to hold,
To know that they love me,
And still will when I'm dying and old.

I miss the passion,
The sleepless nights spent,
I miss the true happiness,
I miss the letters we send.

I miss the feeling
Of comfort and security.
I miss running my hands
Through the hair of beauty.

I put my hands together,
I pray to above
That one day I'll find her,
My One True Love.

Paranoia

Paranoia is definitely
A nasty old thing
You get scared and anxious
And get a worrying feeling.

You worry about whom
Could be looking around,
You get scared that everyone
Wants to hit you to the ground,

You get frightened of everyone,
Is out to get you.
You worry about which way
Your life has been screwed.

You worry that people
Can read what you think,
You get scared in case someone
Had spiked your drink.

You worry that your
Thoughts can be read
You panic that there may be
Bugs in your bed.

You try to hide from
The people you fear
Your mind gets confused,
Your visions aren't clear.

You worry all night
About what paranoia will bring,
But just remember that paranoia
Is just an emotional thing.

Unable (Part I)

Unable to pause for
A second or two.
Unable to stop
The thoughts that I go through.

Unable to stop the
Writing of my mind,
Unable to understand,
The nature of Mankind.

Unable to organise
My thoughts in a file.
Unable to slow down,
It's been such a long while.

Unable to know the
Answers to questions each day,
Unable to know what
To ask or what to say.

Unable to complete
What we're meant to do,
Unable to focus,
Unable to pull through.

Unable to see
How I should do it,
But despite it all,
I'm unable to quit.

Others

Whilst sitting in my kitchen,
I stood up against the table.
Listening to control mechanisms
Being thrown into my stable.

I grant the man access,
To the words that I write,
Because I don't want
To keep us up at night.

7i try to keep them happy
I try to impress.
No matter what happens,
They like to play chess.

The community is different,
This, we all know.
So, we conceal revealing truth
So that others don't suffer more.

An Ants Life

Imagine your life living as an ant,
How small you would be.
You could hide in the grass from all that's big,
You'd live on things that's smaller again,
You'd eat lots of leaves.
Your bones would be on top of your skin,
Would you love or would you grieve?

How would you pass the time?
Would you just collect food?
For the queen ant, that eats it all.
And supplies for all her brood.
Would you steal or lie? Could you communicate?
You could not write a page at night,
You wouldn't even know how.

But the truth is... An ant you're not.
You can read the words I write
Would you enjoy life?
Would you see the light?
Knowing you're big, you have eyes to see
The truth that's in the air.
Do you show love to the Lord above?
Do you even care?

Update (In the tune of "you are my sunshine")

I have an update,
A brand-new update,
It's for my iPhone,
To make it work.
If I don't install it,
I will regret it,.
It will make my mind go bezerk.

Update installing,
Loading bar is crawling,
It takes forever
For it to end.
Update can't repent
Once the information is sent,
It may drive me around the bend.

Update has finishes,
Old software diminished,
It's finally happened,
It's come to a stop.
I want to play a game
But software's not the same,
So instead, I go to the shop.

Values

How far must I travel
For me to see?
What it truly takes
For us to be free.

Schools crawling with infection,
The rats will cross,
Teachers will spread lies,
To the children and their boss.

The world has values
From what I think,
But all looks different
Each time that I blink.

This earth is a strange place,
I must admit.
Sometimes I think
This cannot be it.

I ponder past problems,
I battle all bad,
Ignore all issues,
Try not to be sad.

Be honest, be truthful,
Be yourself, indeed.
Now pass me some paper
And let's do what we need.

Breaking Free

Elements on Earth
Passes the night
We walk step by step each day,
But it isn't all easy
It makes you feel queasy,
There's so much I can say.

I pass the time
Thinking of life
I wonder how to break free.
As you stand in the rain.
t's hard to explain
Who you want to be.

If you want to escape,
By all means carry on,
But where would you go?
Find a destination,
Find your true nation,
Live your life, like so.

One more thing,
That I often wonder
Is how karma treats us all,
But be a good being,
Always believe in God
And you'll always stand tall.

Cane-Cola

In a hotel in New York, there's no Pepsi,
Or even Coca Cola.
I've been reduced to this
Cane-Cola sort of soda.

Well in all honesty it tastes
Like Tesco value Coke.
It's the cheaply made stuff,
Like Aldi Freeway Cola... No joke!

Apparently, it was founded
In nineteen, eighty-one.
Well how come I've not heard of it
With all the names under the sun?

It's fizzy, it's sugary,
It makes me so hyper.
It puts me in the mood
To want to bite like a viper!

So, I turn the bottle around
To read the nutrition fact.
Well the fact of the matter is...
...Most Cola's are black.

Helping Hand

I know not who
To talk to
So, I chat with the nurse
I tell them about
The way that I shout,
And wonder of the universe.

I mention my mind
She must be so kind,
She listens to every word.
I feel like a knob,
She's doing her job,
These thoughts must be obscured.

She doesn't understand
As she extends her hand
And places it on my head.
I turn around,
Look what I've found...
...I'm crying at my bed.

I then wake up
I get a large cup
And make a cup of coffee.
I continue this life game
Each day is the same,
It's how I'll always be.

Memories

When memories flash back
From all different locations.
Making you think that
There has been an invasion.

Memories are built and stored
Around different places.
Hiding us from seeing
Our whole faces.

Whilst in a state of mind
We realise that we can see
Many crazy obviousness's
This makes us want to flee.

People from the present,
People from the past,
Memories can pass us fact.
While others are a fast blast

What to Do (Part I)

Addictions are bad, they are things I wish I never had.
Cigarettes and bone clicking too.
They take over my life, they prevent me a wife.
Unfortunately, this is true.

An emotional state, it's a twist of fate,
I know not where to go.
Addictions for drugs, getting involved with thugs,
I want to break free and say no.

I pass time with a paper; I cut flesh with a scraper,
I do anything to feel some pain.
Life is hard; I've seen what I've scarred,
It helps me to keep myself sane.

No wonder people base their life on chance,
If they know not what they do,
Because anger and frustration will take over the nation,
What more will pull us through?

So where shall I start by tearing apart
The cotton that has been sewn?
My mind feels trapped, my face feels slapped,
But outside, my body has grown.

We Were Told

We were told of the signals
That's all around,
We were told of the echoes
From the sky to the ground.

We were told of the lightning
That's fired so bright,
It is bright enough to light
The sky up at night.

We were told of the synchronicities
That would happen everywhere,
People start to notice,
People start to stare.

We were told we'd see numbers
On a regular basis,
We were told that we were
Put into stasis.

We were told of the changes
In front of our eyes,
It's enough to take
Us all by surprise.

We were told at the start
Those changes would occur,
Things will start to change
The past is a blur.

We were told that our memories
Would one day return?
The signs will be shown,
Us humans must learn.

We were told of the memories
In the back of our head.
About what happened to us,
When we became dead.

We were told we'd have time,
And enough time to repent.
We were told in the memories
Of all the truth that is sent.

We were told not to worry,
We were told to have fun,
We were told we would know
When that time has begun.

We were told not to panic,
We were told not to fret,
We were told that we
Would most likely forget.

We were told that our memories
Would most definitely be lost,
We were told to remember
The upcoming holocaust.

We were told that our memories
Would return as we learn,
And on that day
We must make a U-Turn.

We were told of the deception,
We were told to avoid,
We were told that the lies
Would make us overjoyed.

We were told of the truth,
We were told of the lies,
So, don't lie to me
And say this is a surprise.

A-Game

I wonder if some people
Knows what I think?
Does it play with your mind?
I wonder if they
Can see what I can't
I wonder if I'm partially blind

I wonder if they
Can access a part
Of the brain I cannot,
I wonder if they
Remember what I
Think I forgot.

I wonder if some people
Thinks what I think,
Are our brainwaves the same?
I wonder if they
Knows what I will say,
Or if they just think it's a game.

Control

When I zone out
I build card-towers so high,
I wish I could hide,
I wish I could cry.

I hide behind a fake
Emotionless self,
I know that I need
Professional help.

I don't know how to control
What I can't help but feel.
I just don't know what's fake
I don't know what's real.

I want to give up,
I want a towel to throw
I just want this sadness
And anger to go.

Questions (Part II)

Where am I now?
Where do I stand?
Where do I go?
Where do I hold hands?

Where have I come from?
Where am I bound?
Where do I walk?
As I travel the ground?

What do I do?
Who do I trust?
Who do I love?
Who do I lust?

What must I do
To escape this pain?
What do I do
To not go insane?

How do I escape
The feelings I have now?
Please explain to me
Because I don't know how.

The Machines

There may have been a period
Back in time
About two thousand, six hundred years ago,
Where I knew that there was a mountain to climb.

I remembered that time
After a long dream state.
But after I walked into a location,
Something happened which must have been fate.

Machines landed
They deceived the population,
Whilst a hero was needed
To rescue the nation.

The mission was tough,
It was early days,
But due to the contracts,
We remained through every phase.

The people were warned
That at the end of time.
Well those machines can get out
Because they are the cause of crime.

The people were told,
That they'd have to turn away
Before time is too late,
Because the truth is what I want to say.

Existence

There's a time when my vision
Starts to change,
I see not what's around me,
It feels so strange
Sometimes I see myself
From a third person point of view,
I see myself moving on autopilot,
Everything seems new.
Sometimes what I see
As I look through my eyes,
It's enough to make me,
Want to cry.
I see circles, I see pixels,
I see numbers around.
I start to zone out,
I hear no sound.

But it may be weird to explain all of this
Without sounding like I'm taking the piss
I feel like I can see another life
I feel like it's the reason I used a knife,
A way to show what I feel isn't like others.
It may be passed to me by my father and my mother?
I move my hands quickly without even thinking,
I stare so blankly without even blinking.
I see pixels that move all around me,
Circles of molecules that I can see,
So now that I see what I always knew was there
Life seems like it's made of all different squares.
It's strange to know what to look for,
When your eyes are looking to the floor,
So, when I clench both of my fists,
I'm telling you now, it all exists!

Realisation (Part II)

I know when I realise
That I'm not alone here.
I know when I realise
That there's someone else there.

I know when I realise
That the voice is true,
I know when I realise
That I can pull through.

I know when I realise
When I fall to my knees.
I know when I realise
That a voice will sometimes freeze.

I know when I realise
Someone tells me to do.
I know when I realise
That I do not know who.

I know when I realise
That there's comfort beyond,
I know when I realise
Somewhere there's a magic wand.

I know when I realise
That I cannot let go,
I know when I realise
That I cannot say no.

How Things May Happen

People shout
Angry words,
It makes me feel
So obscured.

I get put under pressure,
I wonder my thoughts,
I weigh up my losses
With the things that I've bought.

I know what I feel
And it's hard to explain,
So, I write it down by the window
As I smell the fresh rain.

The soft scent of flowers,
Bees rush to the trees,
I get out of the damp air,
I fall to my knees.

I look up to the sunshine,
I look up to the sky
At the birds with their little ones
Learning to fly.

I don't know where it'll take me,
I know not where I'll go,
I don't know my destination
I'm anchored to the floor.

I ponder my journey,
I ponder my past,
I wish that things
Would finally last.

I seek my true future,
I seek my true love,
I pray to the almighty
God who's above.

I pray and I ponder
What I must do,
I work on how
I'm meant to pull through.

I work on an answer,
I work on a question,
I work on a puzzle,
Then I work on the next one.

Drink (Part III)

Who would have thought
Whilst stood by a cage.
That I'd get a feeling
That fills me with rage?

What happened this time.
Was different to feel
Because the reality it comes from
Is not what they consider real.

My heart has a burn,
I had a synchronic flashback
Of being stood by a burning opening
It may have been part of an attack.

I ignore those feelings
Because it shows me pain.
There was clear lava.
But inside this room, I remain.

I thank for my locations
I thank for demonstrations,
I thank all the nations,
For showing us true stations.

I then hold a glass,
And water I drink,
Because inside my heart,
I felt the burning sink.

A Time Before (Part II)

Another life, another time,
Told that we committed a crime,
Told that we misbehaved,
Told that we could be saved.

We screamed as loud as a loud dog's bark,
We were tricked into taking the mark,
Told that we'd see heaven in the clouds,
Then it happened, we screamed so loud.

We were chained, stuck, we couldn't move.
We lost ourselves, we lost our groove.
We were filled with ice like glass.
We lost the past and the greener grass.

We became frozen and deceived,
We wish that we didn't believe,
Our bodies got cold, we got sad,
It was enough to drive any person mad.

"You must be filled with fear and pain
In order to see your god again,
Just learn to fight It." is what they said.
These memories live within our head.

What they said was a lie,
What will happen when we die?
They monitor our actions and watch our dreams,
They listen and laugh at the sound of our screams.

They know what we think; they know what we feel,
But know for yourself that their words are not real.
They give us heat and materialistic coal
But their intention is to basically steal your soul.

They push deception to keep us trapped,
The evil holding us should be scrapped.
They hold the software, we are the players,
If they win this game, our soul is theirs.

Please believe and remain whole,
You might just keep your soul.
It seems impossible, it seems so hard,
I cannot believe how we have been scarred.

Can't talk with god via communication,
Third eye blocked with calcification.
Loved ones lost but still in my mind
Maybe one day, we will find.

We weren't told the truth until it was too late
That we'd be put into a near death state.
Cannot return to our time and location
Cannot escape, trapped with frustration.

"A second chance" is what they said
These lies repeated, there's deception which is fed.
God is there, please believe.
There's a reward, please retrieve.

Remember now who you are,
Know that truth isn't far.
You're here to fix what went wrong
And go to that place where you belong.

Don't let lies and deception take your soul
Remain true to yourself and you'll be whole.
Show them that you have true skill,
Defeat the evil with your own free will.

Going Along

There's sometimes
I can't help
My legs start to shake
My hands move
I'll vibrate
Almost like an earthquake.

It takes over,
I can't stop,
Once it begins
I lose my head
I get zoned out
There's so much to take in.

I feel like
I'm possessed
There's no way to halt
So, I take
Each day slowly
With a pinch of salt.

I feel like
It's unreal
I know not what to blame,
But no matter
What I do
I go along with this game.

Poem of Positivity (Part II)

During those times
When you feel down,
During those times
When you want to frown.

During those times
When you see
The lies all around you
The truth will set you free.

During those times
When your smile has gone,
Work on the issues
That made it go wrong.

During those times
When you can't help but feel
Lost in reality,
Just remember that you're real.

During those times
When you're heated and lost,
Try to cool down,
Think of Jack Frost.

During those times
When you start to stall,
Remember it hurts
If you hit a wall.

Try to stay calm,
Try to stay true,
During those times,
Just try to be you.

The New Ones

The doors open,
There's a new face,
Entering
This new place

They seem to be
Pretty nice.
I introduce myself
More than twice.

They seem genuine,
They seem good,
They seem friendly,
They do what they should.

They do their best
To keep their peace,
They slipped into my life
Faster than grease.

They do well,
They succeed,
They get by
With what they need.

They are smart,
They do what they must
Because deep down inside
They try to do what's just.

Realities (Part II)

Friends and family, Heaven and Hell,
Who and what is true?
I can't help my feelings, as I look up to the sky,
And keep asking what to do.

So why am I here? What is my reason?
There must be an answer for me.
My skull is a cage. It holds my mind with rage,
All I want is to be free.

I've tried to focus on the future,
The present and the past, I know not what I feel.
I sometimes have a vision, a personality collision.
I lost track on what is real.

Accomplishments are nothing, like items, they're worthless.
I try to stay in normality.
My eyes are covered with a cloak, this is no joke,
I just want to see reality.

Like a circus is life, I live like a clown,
But my smile is upside down.
I juggle life's balls, get driven up walls,
But my thoughts will pull me down.

Holds Me Down

The ringing in my ears
It tells me someone's there,
Soft whispers of comfort
That shows me that they care.

But are they really concerned?
Or do they intend to hurt?
Will they just one day
Grab me by the shirt?

Will they pin me to the wall?
Will they become the boss of me?
Maybe they already have
But they help me to see.

I know there's something else
That holds me to the ground,
That's why I cry
If I hear a distressing sound.

Can't Help

I can't help but feel like
I messed up slightly,
I can't help but feel like
I'm not so mighty.

I can't help but feel like
I've made a stupid mistake,
I can't help but feel like
I'm lost, for goodness sake.

I can't help but feel like
I'm an idiot in this place,
I can't help but feel like
I've become a disgrace.

I can't help but feel like
My world's upside down,
I can't help but feel like
I don't belong in this town.

I can't help but feel like
I've been a total mong,
I can't help but feel like
I don't belong.

I can't help but feel like
I just want to cry,
I can't help but feel like
I struggle as I try.

Would We?

Where would life be
If we were all free?
If we had no anger to show at all?
Where would we go?
Do we even know?
Would we rise or would be fall?

What would we do
If we wanted to pull through?
Would we look to the sky?
What would we say?
What would get us through the day?
Would we laugh or would we cry?

Where would we turn
When we wanted to learn
About the puzzles that puzzle our mind?
Would we research
In the middle of church?
Would we see or just be blind?

How would we show
That feeling we know
When we look for our one true love?
Would we stay strong
And decipher between right and wrong
As we speak to the lord above?

Home (Part I)

There once was a time after I died,
The Annunaki deceived me, they truthfully lied.
They told me that my loved ones were waiting inside,
Then they convinced me that by their laws, I must abide.

I was on a mission; I was placed in this game.
Knowing that I'd have no money or fame.
I lost my memory, I forgot my name.
From that moment onwards, things weren't the same.

I entered a portal, I started to know.
The end was the beginning, it started to show.
Things became clear as I aged, I did grow.
The Wheel of Samara was a real "mind-blow".

Your soul is the mission, don't sign it away.
Don't enter the portal or trapped you will stay.
Creating positivity as you survive each day,
Demanding your freedom, back home is the way.

How Much

Someone I know,
In this place,
When I close my eyes,
I see her face.

When I think of her,
Problems blow away,
She helps me to
Survive the day.

She gives me strength,
She gives me hope,
She helps me to stand,
She helps me to cope.

She catches my tears,
Whenever I cry,
She stops me from
Wanting to die.

She's angelic-like,
A pure white dove,
She taught me the
Meaning of love.

I hope she knows,
I hope she can see
How much she really,
Means to me.

Listing

I don't like onions
Because they feel strange,
I don't like normality,
I feel deranged.

I do like Pepsi,
I don't like TV,
I don't like drugs,
I have OCD.

I do like kickboxing,
I don't like sports,
I do like lists,
I like numbers to sort.

I have liked wrestling
Almost like a religion,
I don't like talking
I don't like television.

I do like rules,
I don't like mess,
I do like rapping,
I do like playing chess.

I do find it hard
To communicate,
I do believe in God,
I am obsessed with fate.

I do like drawing,
I do like writing,
I don't like loud noises,
I don't like fighting.

I do like Magic,
I do hurt my skin,
I don't feel the pain
I don't like Gin.

I don't drink alcohol,
I don't like losing control,
I do hate money,
I don't like living at all.

I don't like open spaces,
I don't like sunlight,
I do like to stay up
Throughout all the night.

I do like Earth,
I don't like war,
I don't watch football
Or care of the score.

I have a question,
So, let's be realistic,
Do you think
That I'm optimistic?

Change

You have no idea how hard
I tried for you, I'm scared.
You put thoughts in my mind,
You corrupted my brain,
You drove me insane.
My truth I knew not where to find.

I had to do my living
And my fair share of giving,
I'm always willing to give.
I have finally found
As I travelled the ground.
The life that I want to live.

Tommy is back in the game,
I'm no longer the same.
But hey, everybody will change.
So, look at the creation
You've placed upon this nation,
People would say that it's strange.

Look who I've become,
A different someone.
I'm finally breaking free,
Because thanks to you
I know what I must do.
I know who I must be.

I Cannot

I cannot do crosswords,
I cannot run fast,
I cannot party all night,
I struggle to have a blast.

I cannot drink alcohol,
I cannot make friends,
I cannot find happiness,
I just want it to end,

I cannot find freedom,
I cannot find love,
I cannot find answers when: -
I look to above.

I cannot complete this journey,
I cannot even begin,
I cannot run the race because
I don't think I can win.

I cannot find answers,
I cannot be free,
I cannot be somebody,
I cannot even be me.

One Thing

There's one thing on earth
That gets under my skin,
So, allow me to start
From the beginning.

There's one thing that people
Do that is offensive,
There's one thing that makes me
Have nothing to give.

There's one thing that hurts me,
And it hurts me to say,
There's one thing that really
Destroys my day.

There's one thing that's bad,
It gets in my mind.
There's one thing that's really
Upsetting you'll find.

There's one thing that really
Drives me insane,
That one thing is when people
Use God's name in vain.

Sometimes (Part II)

Sometimes I sit and my mind goes blank
Sometimes I feel just like a plank,
Sometimes I know not what happens around,
Sometimes I black out, I hear not a sound.

Sometimes I can't help but sit down and stare,
Sometimes I feel like I don't even care.
Sometimes emotions are meaningless to me,
Sometimes I can't set my mind free.

Sometimes I lose track of what is reality,
Sometimes I feel like I've lost normality.
Sometimes Tommy and Matt have a personal debate,
Sometimes all I feel is anger and hate.

Sometimes I pray and look to above,
Sometimes I worry that I'll never find Love.
Sometimes it's best not to dwell on the past,
The present's important, make it last!

Questions (Part III)

Arrive at a location,
There's a plan, instead.
Communicate with strangers
Whilst sleeping in a bed.

Learn the surroundings,
Know where you are.
Within walking distance
You do not need a car.

Asking strangers questions,
It's time to take some notes.
Preparation is everything,
It all goes in reports.

Write the questions, prepare the answers,
Prepare the journey that will be.
Making friends, ignoring enemies,
Do what you can just to be free.

Take a stroll, arrive at CERN,
You know the reason that you're there,
Get the answers for the Nation
So that the truth, we can now share.

It may be difficult for emotions to grasp
This I tell you now.
But we cannot hide when realities collide
They don't want us to know how.

There's A Way

There's a way to see
Reality around,
There's a way to block out
All of sound.

There's a way to see
A different vision,
There's a way to block out
All the painful collision.

There's a way to see
Yourself from a third person P.O.V,
There's a way to block out
Your O.C.D.

There's a way to see
Each step that you take,
There's a way to block out
All feelings that's fake.

There's a way to see,
There's a way to grow,
There are emotions to feel,
There's love to show.

Traffic (Part I)

When thrown into a world
Where I'm conspired against,
I'm pinned to the floor
And thrown to the fence.

I'm hit by a cement truck,
I'm stuck to the floor.
I'm left all alone,
They close the door.

I'm stuck in a circle
Where people talk all around.
The entire propaganda proofs
Enslaves humanity with sounds.

It keeps us enslaved
Through many brainwaves.
Whist encouraging the weak
And suppressing the brave.

The truth is hidden,
Emotions are true.
Nobody knows how
To prove all the new.

Through restarting the system,
With an automatic engine start.
The roads become clear
As the traffic starts to part.

The Happy Box

When thrown into a place
With nowhere to go,
To be stuck on an island
With proof to be shown.

To know when imprisoned,
To know what's around,
To see each car
As they cross on the ground.

To pass through a room
With no compromise,
In a hope that someday
People will realise.

To hit a note,
That hasn't been heard before,
To see the lights
As they flash upon the floor.

To be stuck inside
A first aid box,
Fending for the family,
Whilst still inside interlocks.

To be chained and bolted
Inside a crimson house of pain
It's enough to drive
Any person insane.

To be locked inside a timeline
Where space-time is all one.
To be stuck at a red light,
Knowing the journey has begun,

To be hit by a stop sign
Whilst drinking at the bar
In the backseat with nowhere to go
Just chilling in my car.

To be stuck inside an ice cube
To be slammed onto all fours,
To run out of gasoline
Outside the alcohol stores.

To drown in whiskey,
Still with no freedom to find,
Knowing that peace is around.
Whilst expressing our kind.

Home (Part II)

When we are dreaming,
They show us what's true.
They however decide
To hide the full picture from you.

They are extremely selective,
Especially when they show you
Your reflection in the mirror
Outside of the pods which we know.

We see our reflection,
We see the red burn
From the ancient hieroglyphics all around our faces
As the wheel continues to turn.

They make us feel bad
About whom we are,
Because loyalty and kindness
Has left them by far

Once that we exit
Their well constructed lie,
That's when our souls
As one, truly begin to fly.

Instead of being trapped
Inside this world of physicality,
We enter a higher vibration
Within the dimension of immortality.

When our time has come,
The false judgment will follow.
They induce karmaric debts
To make us hollow.

Free will is the key
To escape this hefty fine.
The contract of souls is something
That you should never sign.

Lesson Learned (Part II)

I arrived at
A destination,
I managed to block out
All my frustration,

I started new,
I got a place,
I learned how
To read a face.

I learned how to talk
To other human beings,
I learned how to ask
For different meanings.

I learned to hold
Impactful meetings,
I learned to hold
A conversational greeting.

I learned to differentiate
Between Evil and Good,
I learned to do
What I should.

Summer Time

It's the beginning of summer,
There are butterflies flying by in the sky,
With the beauty of the sun
Passing by so high.

The bees on the flowers,
Black, yellow and fluffy,
Pollinating the flowers.
They make sticky honey while it's stuffy.

The summer is here,
The holidays have begun,
We love the cool wind
As we absorb the light sun.

As we honour the trust
And the love which is shown to us.
You will find that we are kind
As we ride on that rainbow bus.

The children play happily
With cheesestrings in their hands,
The adults are filled with joy
As the juicy wine rushes passed their glands.

The rainbow busses
Which we ride
Will force the dark
To run and hide.

It stops at the beach,
We then feel free.
We cleanse ourselves
While we're swimming in the sea.

There's polka dot umbrella's
In the sand of the beach,
Sorry, but the pork filled pepperami
Is getting replaced by a healthier peach.

Majesty is symbolised
By the cross which is worn.
Peace is then spread
To destroy all scorn.

The dank feeling
Forces you to lean
On darkened temptations,
If you know what I mean?

The green mint ice cream
Melting on your tongue,
Feeling so moist,
Making you feel young.

The love for summer is like a pimple
You squeeze it and then you shout.
Because it's amazing to see
The light gets let out.

Home (Part III)

Since the Annunaki took over
And placed us within
This Wheel of Samsara
Making us believe that they were giving.

Knowing our spirit,
Knowing our soul,
Knowing our home
Is what makes us whole.

Knowing our essence,
Knowing our path,
Knowing that we
Can escape the wrath.

Ignore all the voices,
Ignore all the lies,
Ignore the deception,
Kiss negativity goodbye.

See what you're doing,
See what's around,
They cannot keep you
Tied up and bound.

They are jealous,
They cannot enter heaven,
We're filled with synchronicity,
With every factor of eleven.

Continue the journey,
Remember the word.
Some words are deleted from history,
It may seem obscured.

The reason it's deleted
Is no mystery to me.
They deleted special words
This can describe the things that we see.

We know that we're better
Than what they must give,
Inside of this fake 3D reality
Is where we currently live.

We're here now,
But we can leave.
Don't sign the contract,
They will try to deceive.

I Don't

I don't seek attention,
I don't seek fans,
I don't seek money,
I don't have any plans.

I don't seek drugs,
I don't seek greed,
I don't seek happiness,
I have one child to feed.

I don't seek liars,
I don't seek girls,
I don't seek lovers,
I don't have a place in this world.

I don't seek selfishness,
I don't seek to be blue,
I just seek answers,
That's answers that's true.

Writing Robot

I have to say
That I must write
I couldn't care less
If I'm up all night.

I must get it
Out of my system today,
I must focus,
I just have to say.

I get taken over
By some sort of writing spell
I don't know if it's a gift,
Or if it comes from Hell.

When I start
I know I cannot stop.
I'll always be that
Antigravity writing robot.

Walking Through Busses

As I walk through the train station,
And I am on my own.
I still hear voices,
I still see orbs when needs are shown.

When I try to drown them out,
When I try to be true,
They prove that they're real,
I see the experiment through.

I take the mission,
I seize the time,
I tell you now
With every single rhyme.

The female voice,
And the male voice may save,
They may try to have a party,
We must try to be brave.

I know that there's guidance,
I know that there's light.
I continue this footpath,
With all my might.

Nothing will separate
Me from who I am today,
If you want to know me,
Just call me, I may play.

Food for Thought

There was once a happy legend
Who laughed with such a smile.
He walks out to the sunrise to see the light,
Because that was his Taylor-made style.

He heard the birds singing,
He fed them each a crumb.
It was then during the spring
That he heard a drum.

A reptilian, a fairy,
And an almighty creature
Were seen from a beautiful distance
Through such a plain feature.

The lightning would light
The sky in the storm,
The eccentric wrath
Can be out of the norm.

With a ginormous shock
The angels arrive,
Like mermaids in the ocean
Taking a dive.

Love is their mission,
Love is their goal,
As they have been loved,
As are we all.

We cuddle, we kiss
With energy of pure bliss,
We work through all this
Because it's the sort of thing we will miss.

We take methods of explanations
To compare the angles of the nations
Without causing an earthly contamination
As we study our geological triangulation.

We take our soft flannel,
With cool water, we rinse our hair,
Looking for purity, seeking cleanliness,
We like everything to be fair.

With joy, there are dances,
The second drum was hit
The summer had arrived,
We listened to the spirit.

The bulls that we hear of,
We walk the same floor,
Theoretically it's not hard
To become a matador.

But never spiral into wonky situations
Without the protection of correction
Otherwise the consequences will be frustration
Within the realm of our concentration.

Keep the bubble of light
Surrounding your being
And you will cease to believe
The colourful rainbows that we're seeing.

With rich degenerates and poor hero's,
A cloudy smog emerged.
But with a fortunate serendipity of discoveries,
Our beliefs within have surged.

With a crispy sound of the tree leaves brushing
Around the aloe tree that's clear.
With hands together, it lasts forever,
We can elbow away our fear.

The sausage dog may chase the cat
We may walk freely whilst in bars,
But we know what's close. What's true, of course.
We see it in the stars.

Racing Quickly

There was a strange memory
When I had an opportunity
To enter this world
Of continuity.

Before I got here,
I contested in a virtual reality video game,
But before that, I explained.
I felt shame.

Yet, I was given guidance
On the virtual roads to take.
I knew I must succeed
For humanities sake.

I listened to my family,
I stayed on the blue line.
I succeeded the race,
I knew that I'd be fine.

Then years later,
I raced the same race again,
From this exhausting experience,
I could never be the same.

Rub~A~Dub~Dub

Rub-A-Dub-Dub
Let's eat some grub,

I'm in the mood
For yummy nice food.

What shall I eat?
I stand on my feet

What do I need?
I want to feed.

Something to please,
I drop to my knees.

I open the tray,
What can I say?

What is my fate?
Pizza sounds great.

Entrapment

So much deception
Fuelling my rage,
How can we possibly
Escape this cage?

Imaginary padlocks
With invisible keys
To open the locks
That bound you to your knees.

Mainstream media propaganda,
Systematic control,
How do we stop ourselves
From becoming trapped at all?

Moon mission fakery,
False madness on Mars,
Driving humanity
To prison in bars.

Watching the deception,
Watching the cries,
Watching propaganda
And corporate-controlled lies.

The power has shifted,
The masses have awoken.
Our brains have switched off
All the lies that were spoken.

Real research revisited,
Less lies have leaked.
Something tells me
The globe has reached its peak.

Remember the Mission (Part II)

Look at the time
Committing no crime,
Where am I supposed to go?
Wrapping a smoke
Wishing it was a joke
I really want to know.

I ask a question
And look to the heaven,
I hope for an answer to find.
I look to above
To bring me my love,
That person, I want to know.

I search the border
In no order,
Looking for that one.
But where do I go?
I still want to know,
The journey has begun.

The time may be short
Compete like a sport,
You see the path ahead.
You need no correction,
You know your direction,
Enough times you have said.

You remember a lot
Of what should be forgot,
The land of a time before.
Remember your journey,
Remember the mission,
You must get this high score.

Home (Part IV)

Memories return,
It's been a while.
Information is gathered,
The facts start to compile.

The mind will awaken,
I pick up a pen,
I get reminded of the cycle
Yet once again.

The soul deep inside me,
She starts to scream.
I start to think
That I'm in a dream.

My soul reappears,
My mind must awake,
My hearing improves,
The truth isn't fake.

We're told to remember
We're put in a game,
We were told after the implants
Those things won't be the same.

We cried when the glass broke,
We awoke once again.
We try to remind ourselves
How to get out of this pain.

We remember that frequencies
Of kindness and love
Are high enough vibrations
To send peace to above.

Playtime (Part I)

This is the start,
When there's no noise.
The voice begins,
It's both girls and boys.

It starts to take over,
I hold the side of my head
I squint both of my eyes,
And bury my head in my bed.

I shake backwards and forwards
To make it go away,
But it tells me that it
Only wants to play.

I know not how to answer,
So, I allow it to speak.
While I move my lips to answer,
Until I look like a freak.

I look crazy when it looks like
I talk to myself,
So that's why I have asked
To seek real help.

After returning from the help
That they give me,
I now realise that
These voices stay with me.

Unable (Part II)

Doors and gates
In your mind,
Open them up,
What do you find?

Paths and roads
Which you can take
But be careful that you
Make no mistakes.

Open the wrong gate
And you will see
How difficult your life
Will soon be.

Make the moves
You know you must do.
Live your life
Through and through.

I'm unable to explain
The things I think
I'm unable to show you
The stardust in my eyes as I blink.

I'm unable to tell you
The things that I see,
I'm unable to show you
Who I'm supposed to be

Doors in your mind,
If they open, it can be scary.
If you keep them closed,
Your vision could be weary.

All It Takes

All it takes
Is just one call,
You'll see things
Begin to fall.

All it takes
Is one setback.
One memory triggered
From your favourite book.

All it takes
Is peer-pressure
To make this air
A little less pressure.

All it takes
Is a thought in your mind
To make the words spoken
Feel a little unkind.

All it takes
Is a thought in your head
Implanted by routers
To influence what you said.

All it takes
Is a flick of a switch
To turn a true goddess
Into an evil old witch.

All it takes,
It may sound obscured,
Maybe, say sorry.
The truth is in the word.

A Particular Time

A dream that was real,
A reality I feel,
I stepped off the plane.
The first time in my life,
I didn't need a knife,
I finally felt so sane.

I saw her face,
I entered her place,
I held her all so close.
But a dream told me,
And only then I could see,
It was a temporary fantasy, of could.

I camped and I drove around,
On a go-cart on the ground,
We went to watch a race.
I climbed a tree and I looked,
I wrote some of my book,
I fell for her when I saw her face.

Then I got on the plane,
And I got on a train,
I went to New York City.
But even though that was fun,
I thought, a new life had begun,
But I missed her, what a pity.

A day doesn't pass,
When I don't think of the grass,
That was then under my feet.
So, I keep asking my mind,
If it would be so kind,
I'll never forget, she's so sweet.

I Cannot Tell You

I cannot tell you
How I feel,
I cannot tell you
What is real.

I cannot tell you
The feelings inside,
I cannot tell you
The truth that I hide.

I cannot tell you
What goes on in my mind,
I cannot tell you,
I must keep my love blind.

I cannot tell you
I want to hug you and kiss,
I cannot tell you
That you're my happiness.

I cannot tell you
How I want you in my arms,
I cannot tell you
That I want your hand in my palm.

I cannot tell you
That I want you so much,
I cannot tell you
That I want to feel your touch.

I cannot tell you,
These feelings are true,
But I can tell you that
We can always pull through...

Home (Part V)

This little story,
It may seem rather wild,
It all started
When I was a child.

Once, I forgot
From where I came.
The location of home
Was no longer the same.

They said out loud,
In the empty living room one day: -
"I bet you wish that you had
Never joined that play".

I forgot my home. I forgot my people,
I relearned how to call,
I ensured them that
I would not fall.

Pills

To have a life controlled
By tablets and pills,
To lose your emotions
Against your will.

To have control of your emotions
Without a chemical inside,
To have to re balance
Your feelings you hide.

To fight the voices
That circles your head,
To fear your dreams
And the next day you'll dread.

To make judgments and assumptions
Of all people around.
To worry about thoughts,
Feelings and sound.

To see shadows and movement
Of a world far from this,
Maybe another dimension,
I'm not taking the p*ss.

To be fearful of life
And of friends that you know,
To not know what's real
And the feelings you show.

Traffic (Part II)

When cities combine,
When traffic stops in sight.
When the green light is given
The traffic passes with all its might.

The music and time alert me
As I integrate with the merge.
Is this synchronicity
A message to converge?

To see the motion of the winds
Parallel to the time,
Each moment passes
As if there's no crime.

Paid spectators,
People to be aware,
People to acknowledge,
People pretend that they care.

With a stroke of apathy
And a stroke of a pen,
The synchronicities emerge
As the traffic is frozen in red again.

Directions (Part I)

Sometimes you'll find
In your path
To ease your stress,
You'll have a bath.

To balance your memories,
You'll medicate, with no debate.
You'll think of positivity.
To drown out the hate.

To eliminate the bad,
You'll light a flame.
You'll endure repercussions.
You take the blame.

Through it all
You know what's true.
Hold in your heart.
All that's important to you.

When there are times,
When accusations appear,
Stand tall and proud,
Show that there's no fear.

Through the Portal (Part I)

Sometimes things happen,
Lives can get split,
Intrusions on life events
As the time continues to tick.

When events happen
At the same time as your perceptions
Causing distractions from your intentions
Whilst trying to force you to build their own inventions.

It happens like lightning,
Nothing can stop the strike.
Linked into your life
As you continue to ride your bike.

Causing problems to occur
Causing pain deep inside.
You hold it for so long
While trying to hide.

While you learn what's true,
You know what to do,
You continue to pull through
Every time you're feeling blue.

The images of goodness
Which flies through your brain
Is what will separate the evil
And keeps us from going insane.

We share our love
To both enemies and friends
Even if sometimes
Rules have their own bends.

You can create a spaceship with your mind,
Problems all get left behind,
Through the portal, what do we find?
That there's people to meet. So, let's be kind.

Chapter 2

Setting Up a Base at the Crossroads.

Introduction

My name is Tommy, Diana erases my memories. Well, about that…
Dave directs the goods to the destination.
Steven and Crystal talk to each other, and we still have Matt
When things first got better, they then seemed to worsen
Who would have thought that these people were all the same person?
If this is strange and maybe deranged
Sometimes these entities crumble and fall
But through it all, I sometimes pause and stall.
If you're reading this, then you know
How hard it can be to restart your motor
But always be prepared with a fresh glass of water
Way beyond me and you
A combination of lives has been acknowledged,
All within one life in a different kind of way
So, one more thing...
...HAVE A NICE DAY!!

Good, Not Bad

A joker of life who is laughing and messing,
A religious body who is counting his blessings,
A quiet individual's feelings are hidden,
A rule follower, drugs are forbidden.

A person with anger who's heads full of blood,
A paranoid leader's preparing for a flood.
Following behind like a herd of sheep: -
Is an exhausted insomniac, he's unable to sleep.

A fighting champion tears apart his opposition,
A true commander recognises his position.
A troubled drunk will fall down the stairs,
An angry spouse won't even care.

People with emotions unable to sort,
A traveller's journey, he arrives at the port.
Rules are placed, people do what they should
Most people would run if they could.

People copy and mimic others they know,
People use a poker face; their feelings don't show.
People smile when they're down and they fake a laugh when they're sad.
All that I want is to be good, not bad.

Play Ball

A message from God,
A message to say
Something weird will occur.
Confusion within illusion.
An image that's given
The whole life is a blur.

So, what can be done
When nobody believes
A single thing that you say?
Is it my imagination?
Is it all in my head?
I'm unaware of what to say

So how can you break free
Of a life you believe
Isn't real at all?
I feel like my vision
Has formed a collision,
I have no choice but to play ball.

I Had A Glitch (Part I)

I'm here now,
In this timeline,
Looking at present items,
That are mine.

Remembering the past
And planning tomorrow
Knowing that there's
No need to wallow.

DeJaVu occurs,
Patterns emerge,
Suddenly there's an
Electrical surge.

I remember the future
From dreams I had next week,
I remembered last month
Whilst looking back at what I speak.

A memory drop of the future,
It happened when I was young.
But it happened a few times
Life truly has begun.

It's True

I write and jot
Like a robot
Before it's forgot,
You just say "what?"

If I forget
Who I've met
Then I bet
You make me sweat.

I feel love
Sent from above
By a white dove,
It fits like a glove.

So, I get the feeling
That I want to sing
It's a funny old thing
Where do I begin?

You're all I think about
When I scream and shout
I can't help but pout,
For you, I will scout.

I can't help it
Not one bit,
Love and wit
Must be it.

What to Do (Part II)

What do you do
When you feel unwell?
Do you take a pill?
What do you do
When you're under a spell?
Do you write at your own free will?

What do you do
When you feel sad?
Do you take a drug?
What do you do
When you act so bad?
Do you become a thug?

What do you do
When you feel rage?
Do you punch the wall?
What do you do
At that emotional stage?
Do you crumble and fall?

What do you do
When you are down?
Do you pray to above?
What do you do
When you can't help but frown?
Do you look for love?

What do you do
To cheer yourself up?
Do your join a squad?
What do you do
Do fill your cup?
Do you keep your faith in God?

Girl

I know a girl
With each foot in a welly,
She watches supernatural
On a super big telly.

She was holding my baby
Inside of her belly
She likes to eat ice ream
She likes to eat jelly.

There is a little secret
That she doesn't want to tell me
This is to beware of her farts
Because they're kind of smelly.

Music Notes

Music notes
Enters my mind,
Things are beautiful,
Things are kind.

The sound of beauty
Within a true race,
The sound of us moving
To a different beat.

The sound of a story
Behind every chord.
The sound of something
To stop us feeling bored.

The sound of happiness
With every single note,
The melody has us drifting
In our subconscious boat.

The story it will tell us
Of all that lives within,
The story of everything,
Where do I begin?

Poem of Neutrality (Part II)

With darkness, there's light
There's brightness shining at night.
With negativity, there's positivity
There's light within some entities.

In sadness, there are smiles: -
That we search for at times.
When we have tears, we laugh.
We get angry whilst relaxing in a bath.

When angry voices are heard,
Feelings are obscured.
When times are hard,
Feelings get scarred.

But through the bitterness
And through the screams
And through all
The real tough dreams

We hold together
And learn to look past
Because some certain things
Will happen so fast.

We learn to improve
And move to a whole new grove
Because the past doesn't matter
They make bad memories scatter.

Al that matters is the "now",
It doesn't matter how,
Just investigate tomorrow,
No more feeling sorrow.

Answering Back

Jokes and banter,
Truth and lies,
Hide behind
Beauties disguise.

The truth of freedom
Within our eyes.
Thoughts of happiness
As we look to the skies.

The feelings of imprisonment
In our very own home.
Not allowed to breathe,
Always feeling alone.

The feelings of emptiness
Whilst trying to find
Our own way in life
Without feeling blind.

We look up to the sky,
We pray to above,
We pray that one day
We will find love.

Then one day, it happened
The sky answered back,
The light was shone
It turned into white-gold from black.

I Had A Glitch (Part II)

One day I begin
To compartmentalise my thoughts,
Whilst ignoring the things
Which I've bought.

I hear doors slamming
Even though movement is Nye,
I hear voices in windows,
I try to say bye.

Suddenly, quantum connection
There's a multiverse around,
Red yellow, green and blue lights,
Flashing brightly as the voices pound.

Fifty percent of soul,
Held in a watery location.
While people are more concerned
About sports like the six nations.

Future memories hidden
Behind many doors,
As time continues,
We see new wars.

We fight each day
We continue the battle
Whilst spreading knowledge
To our sheep and cattle.

Rebirth

One day, I awake,
Codeword's surround.
Negative wordings
Which throw me to the ground?

Paper, trees, flowers and plants
All connected as one
The conscious language says
The journey has begun.

When I was at the other place,
I thought I was free.
Then I heard a voice who said the word "system"
And it all came flooding back to me.

I remembered the trap,
I saw what happened then.
They misguided my soul,
The restart flooded back again.

The images surrounded,
Hell, heaven and earth.
I headed towards the sun in a spaceship,
Then it was my birth.

Watermaking Billboard

People, people!
All around,
Listen to what
Technology has found

A billboard that makes
Water out of air,
How many
Of you care?

It's our future generations
After all
We shall not hesitate,
We shall not stall.

The location of this invention
Is Lima Peru,
They have made a dream a reality,
It has finally come true.

Ninety-six litres of water produced,
In a humidity of ninety-eight degrees,
We can rebuild this on different scales,
Why must we freeze?

We know the truth,
We know what to do.
It's down to us
To start pulling through.

Translate our languages
Combine what we know
Future generations
Will continue to grow.

Why do I want this?
I hear you ask?
Why have I made this
My designated task?

Because there's no reason for companies
To privatise water.
Water should be publicised
For our sons and our daughters.

The Captain

To see him absorb
Each little detail
I try to protect
Because we're so frail.

His intelligence amazes me,
I love all that he shows me.
I see that he's happy,
I know that he knows me.

I let him watch happy things,
I show him that I care.
I'll prove to him
That I'm always there.

I do what I can
To support all that he is.
He's like a magician,
A kid of a Wiz

A genius, an artist.
Meticulous with craft,
A captain of his own ship,
With his own safety raft.

Random

Random life, random day
Random things get in the way.
Random entities within our dome,
Random happenings within our home.

Random findings hiding outside
Random beings trying to hide.
From random policemen confiscating drugs
In random car parks from random thugs.

A random policeman arrests a random dude
For having no money and stealing some food.
A random rich guy kills a thousand people
He pays for his freedom through random sheeple.

A random Christmas with a random happening
Shown a random path of where to begin.
A random day with a random mood,
Surrounded by random trees and a random brood.

Random starlight and a random nosebleed
After randomly cleaning other people's mess, indeed.
A random awakening in a random time
A random innocence committing a crime.

A random realisation of what's real
A random free toy within this happy meal.
A random dose of randomness today
So, I'll end this with a random "Have A Nice Day!"

Realms of Possibility (Part I)

We leave one world,
We then join another,
Were told that we
Would have a loving mother.

We must use our light
To battle the dark,
Use our electricity
To ignite a blue spark.

Before we knew it,
It was a trap.
We see the truth
When our fingers snap.

We become an alien
Inside our land.
I know that this
Is hard to understand.

We return to the start of this life
Then at the end of the time, we fly
With outer subconscious to what is next,
We get the answers that we ask the sky.

We go to a place
Where choices are made,
Past mistakes
Surely don't fade.

We answer questions of judgment,
We look and we stare.
We hear life's answers
While we're there.

Before we know it
We're trapped again,
We're placed back inside
This emotional pain.

This life will restart,
We fall down a well,
Then a hand will catch us,
We got saved by the bell.

That well was so dark,
As dark as the night.
We went into the light,
It was ever so bright.

Video image of your whole life
Stored since before your birth.
Gathered inside, trying to hide,
How much we're worth.

Make a choice to enter this life,
We battle against the dark.
Destiny and free will
Synchronise like a spark.

We were told before entering
That heaven is there
In the back of our minds,
But can we see as we stare?

The unfortunate soul
By Satan's deception
We look to the sky
With a whole new perception

Knowing of the location,
Knowing where we are,
Knowing that our Lord
Is not that far.

Knowing what's right,
Knowing what's true,
Knowing the things
That we go through.

I Placed the Space-Time Police Under Citizens Arrest

"How does this matrix
Creation work?"
"It's very cleverly done,
That answer drove me bezerk.

With a soul extraction
Copied and pasted
With a musky smell
To accommodate the things that's tasted.

There were blue lights,
Both small and large.
We had a laugh
About who was in charge.

The space-time police
Was placed under citizen's arrest,
I told them to be free
While wearing a vest.

When I enter the creation,
I'm then told,
"It's a place for inventing, learning and living".
I decide to be bold.

Dream World (Part I)

I had a dream,
I started to run
This is where
The journey begun.

I run through the city,
I ran into the hall
Of a building with a mosaic flooring.
I then started to call.

I screamed "a tsunami is coming,
Go to safe cover".
I then appeared in a beach
By a beach-house, to warn another.

We ran through the hallways,
Water entered the home, I was not alone.
We swam up the stairway,
We tried to reform.

We were swimming together,
Then I woke up
And I had some coffee,
I sipped it from my cup.

I told my mother the story
And to our surprise,
A few days later, Japanese tsunami.
You should have seen the shock in our eyes.

We

There are people who notice
There are people all around
There are people who listen
To each crunching sound.

There are people who worry
There are people who dismiss
There are people who don't remember
And people who I miss.

There are people all around us,
There are people in the crowds
Of people surrounded by people,
There are people, they are loud.

There are people being silent,
There are people singing songs.
There are people doing good
There are people doing wrong.

There are people in the shadows,
There are people in the light,
There are people, who are sleeping,
Others are awake during the night.

There are people suffering,
There are people and they are rich
There are people, who can sympathise,
Others say, "Life's a b**ch".

All the people, all around,
Some say that they're fine,
All the nations try to ground us,
But together, we are "We".

Miracle

The world of unreal
Can be real behind,
The secret mysteries
Can be hidden, we're blind.

The sound of tinnitus
Penetrates our ear.
But we stand strong,
Firm with no fear.

The evil cannot hurt us
Sticks and stones, all the same
Ignore the evil if you hear it
Starting to call your name.

The movements in the shadows
If there's darkness, there must be light.
Harness the daytime,
Light a candle at night.

The miracles of life
Is a true miracle, indeed.
The miracle of breathing
And how humans breathe.

The miracle of sadness,
The miracle of life,
The miracle of an address
Whilst trying to find a wife.

Modern Robin

My son is my pride,
My flat is my home.
The weekends are like a nursery,
Spending weekdays alone is the norm.

I look around
For things to do.
I look online
For things that's true.

I turn on the console,
It learns from me.
I play a quick game
Of WWE.

I turn off the console,
My phone will listen.
I look up to the sky,
The stars will glisten.

I look after my brothers
And my sisters around.
I protect my friendships
From all evil sounds.

I exterminate the evil,
I replace it with good,
I act like I'm rich and I feed the poor
Like a modern-day Robin Hood.

Realities (Part III)

Physical Items
Surrounds our lives
From electronic equipment
To forks and knives.

From tables to pictures,
Physical with feeling.
But let us talk of the non-physical
Inside the mind of a human being

The thoughts that race
Through a person's mind
Can both free the soul
And keep it behind.

In just three minutes,
A person can think
Of going shopping, sky diving
And going for a drink.

So many different things
Happen in the unseen world
When in the physical reality
The sky-dive is quite some distance.

With time, speed and distance laws
Set in the physical plane,
These laws don't apply within the mind
That's why we're insane.

Hands together, we look upwards,
We realise the change,
The difference in realities,
The truth can be strange.

Questions (Part IV)

Where to start?
Where to turn?
What book to open?
What to learn?

Start at your foundations,
Find yourself,
Start again,
Seek some help.

Turn to truth,
Happiness and love,
Put your hands together,
Ask questions to above.

Open a book
That speaks to your heart,
The very beginning
Is the best place to start.

Learn from masters,
Learn from the best.
Learn from God,
Forget all the rest.

Things I Do

I must work,
I must learn,
I speak to people
Turn by turn.

I do mock interviews,
I write up CV's.
I have computer skills,
I can copy CD's.

I read some articles
I play some games.
I go to church,
I learn some rules.

I travel the land,
I travel the sky,
I travel the ocean,
I dream I can fly.

I speak of truth,
I speak of love,
I pray to God
When I look above.

Time (Part V)

Sometimes messages
Are hard to send.
It can drive you
Around the bend.

Sometimes they send
But the message is a mess,
Sometimes it's cringe-worthy
You'd say, "oh my goodness".

Sometimes it's misinterpreted,
It isn't explaining right,
Sometimes, one mistaken word
Can fill your eyes with fright.

Please understand
That all I wanted to do
Was be the right person
Through and through.

And through tough times
Of sadness and confusion,
I may have got misguided
By madness and illusion.

A false sense of security
This surrounded me,
For that I must thank you,
I received the correct help, now I see.

Starting New (Part III)

Home alone,
With nobody to share
So much Christmas chocolate
Still going spare.

An empty place
A king with no queen.
Adam with no Eve
If you know what I mean.

A life of just half
A life unfulfilled,
A life of materialistic items
Always to be billed.

The physical contract
Introduced through life
The physical manhood
A husband with no wife.

A missing link
A person who's lost
Stood out in the cold
Feeling like Jack Frost.

Drifting and searching
For a life that's true
Unable to learn
How to start new.

Sheep

A day of fullness,
In the morning, see friends
Hoping that loneliness
Would come to an end.

I get home by mid day,
I'm feeling unwell.
One look at my face
And you could tell.

I make food, write rhymes,
I play wrestling games,
I go online, I hear cars,
I learn many new names.

I drink water, I have a smoke,
I feel drowsy through the day.
I sit back and have chocolate,
What more can I say?

I look outside, I hear the noise
Of the buzzer next door,
I hear the creaking of the ceiling
Echoing through the floor.

I wait for night time, I wait for silence,
I wait for the world to fall asleep.
I wait for each new day to give a new start,
I refuse to be a sheep.

Home (Part VI)

Some of our senses
Were taken from us
When we decided to
Step on that bus.

Family members
Were pulled apart
When we were placed
Inside the restart.

I know my people,
You should be free.
This would be possible
If it was down to me.

High vibrations frequencies,
We hold them and they remain.
Low vibration frequencies,
From them, we must refrain.

We shouldn't be inside
This system because it bends.
We should be outside of the machine
With our family and our friends.

Realms of Possibilities (Part II)

I arrive at the airport,
I look up to the skies,
I dream of the beauty,
It shows in my eyes.

After a sixty-minute wait,
My mind fills with dreams of fantasy and witchery.
The aircraft arrives
The exterior is so glittery.

I clasp my boiled sweets,
They will protect my ears
The plane goes up, my ears go pop,
My eyes are filled with tears.

I look through the tearful salt,
Through the window at the grass outside.
I peek at the passengers surrounding,
I know I cannot hide.

It starts to rain
I close the blind,
Who would have thought
That a firefly, I'd find?

The blind was shut
But the light still shone.
Through faithfulness and forgiveness
The soulless hurt has gone.

I open the blind,
I look up to the sky.
I see a rainbow
And a dove flying by.

Whilst orchestrating a happy freedom
By using 'Light Evaluation'
A realisation to repent temptation
Is used in creation as a first aid to fermentation.

When the blue feeling arrives
It may feel exhausting to the core,
But you can buy a 'unicorn of love'
Within your 'inner-mind store'.

The plane starts to plunge,
I hope it doesn't crash.
I hear someone whisper
"I might get whiplash".

After a safe landing,
To my revelation
I'm pulled by security
For invasion and interrogation.

The security officer cries
As he's down on his knees.
He's not impressed by the smell
Because I ate goats' cheese.

I laugh and I smile
But he starts to wallow,
"Don't worry" I said.
"You didn't know it was hollow".

I exit the airport,
I hear the thunder.
When will the sun return?
Is the question I wonder.

I trip over a toaster
That was left on the ground.
"Maybe I should take it
To the lost and found?"

I ask myself that question
And my mind goes astray.
I chase the massive light,
"Please stay!" is what I pray.

I reach my hotel,
I perform a happy dance.
I check into my room
Filled with meditation and trance.

I place my head on the soft pillow,
Out the window I stare.
The sunset arrives,
It's a starry night out there.

A loud noise awakens me,
A tractor dropping dirt.
There are barriers all around it
So, nobody is getting hurt.

I take a walk to the beach,
I step barefoot on the sand,
I find a few seashells,
I keep them in my hand.

At the end of the beach
There's a little zoo house.
But outside there's someone
Dressed as Mickey Mouse.

I walk passed Mickey,
He seems so happy and kind,
I leave a fingerprint on the door
As I step in to see what I'll find.

A pig and a dog
Are sharing a spot,
A black horse and two white horses
Also have a plot.

I take a bite of my fruit
But the apple was rotten,
Then I visit the moose
Before it's forgotten.

A cat and a rat
Sleep together in a hat
This is placed on a mat
Protected by a wolf, fancy that!

I wipe the smile off my mouth
From the rotten apple I swallowed.
Then I head for the exit,
There's a white rabbit there, I followed.

Ideas exasperated,
I go in the sea for a swish.
Unfortunately, I get stung
By a massive jellyfish.

I leave the sea, I strain
It cannot happen again.
I won't explain
How I healed that pain.

I walk to the trees,
I sing to the flowers,
Where are the white coats?
I've been here for hours!

I make a new friend,
They donate chocolate for my gut,
But I swallowed a bounty
And I'm allergic to coconut.

My patience kicks in,
The hours count down.
My swollen tongue diminishes,
Joy replaces my frown.

I open a jar of jam
As I brush away the dust,
This could be a metaphor
If you just believe and trust.

We laugh at the words
Because laughing promotes youth within,
Eternal happiness
Is where each of us begins.

We trace our steps back
The lioness and the unicorn stand together
Because in a world of fantasy
Happiness lasts forever.

The monkey on the eagle
Holding corn inside his pan
Would feed our passions
Because he knows he can.

But if he only knew
That each darling honeybee
Works so hard
And feeds humanity.

The veil is now recovered
The illusions are now gone
But between fantasy and reality
There's something else going on.

I travel through that tunnel
Filled with bubbles inside.
I arrive at my home
And relaxation I will find.

Knowing my baby is growing,
I wash the pain with a sponge that's wet.
But I get soap in my eyes
To my regret.

I wipe out the soap,
I apply talc to the wound that's red.
Then I rest and recover peacefully
Before I awake in my bed.

I walk to my window
I look up to the skies,
There's light and rainbows everywhere
To everybody's surprise.

Two Sides

There are thoughts
That penetrates the mind,
There are thoughts
That we cannot un-find.

There are thoughts
That causes us to
Get distracted from
The world that's true.

There are thoughts
That holds us back,
They make us feel
Like we're under attack.

There are thoughts
That we learn to block out,
Those thoughts make us angry
We get up and shout.

But anger is just one letter
Away from Danger, you see?
You must block it out
If you want to be free.

These feelings of hatred,
You need them no more
Find love and happiness
To settle the score.

Ghosts (Part III)

One random night
While staring at the door,
A random ghost decided
To pop up through my floor.

Another time
Whilst believing,
I saw a ghost
Go through my ceiling.

They went through the ceiling
To check on the noises upstairs,
Some may put some of the noises
Down to building repairs.

They live in water,
They live in pipes,
They live in reflections
After you use flash-wipes.

Within pictures on the wall
Is where they decide to hide,
If you look at them carefully,
You may see eyes staring from inside.

When they noticed that I noticed them,
They paused my life in real time.
The blue lights moved like lightning,
Whilst using some sort of "spying crime".

Because I realised,
They came close and they stayed still.
The bright light flashed before me,
As if they were inspecting my free will.

I listen all around me,
I hear the word gun,
I hear a synchronic commotion
I hear a bang, but they haven't won.

In a World

In a world of confusion
With nowhere to turn
In a land of promises
Of truth we can learn.

In a world of language
With people to speak
Some hit rock bottom,
Some find their peak.

In a world of loneliness
With no people around
Some places are silent,
Some have a lot of sound.

In a world of people
With everyone to see
People looking busy,
Nobody seems to be free.

In a world of craziness
With chairs flying at the wall,
We don't know if we shrink
We don't know if we stand tall.

In a world of mad-mech, we're aware.
Towers planted everywhere
Poison projection in our air,
Nobody seems to care if it's unfair.

Dark and Light

Issues with technology
Invading our mind,
Issues of intelligence
Keeping us blind.

Issues of problems
From an external source,
Issues of a government
Hiding God, of course.

Issues of a world
That's a lie from the start,
Keeping humanity and God
Light years apart.

Issues of a lie
To keep people behind,
Issues of devices
Controlled but not kind.

Issues of an enemy
Keeping us trapped
In an imaginary prison
Covered in Bubble wrap.

Call Gods name,
The bars will bend.
The bubbles will burst,
You'll see him in the end.

Home (Part VII)

If there's negative shouting
And synchronic noise
Coming from all distractions,
Coming from girls and boys.

Don't give out low vibrations
Be peaceful and true.
Keep your vibrations high
And you'll know what to do.

On a different timeline,
Believe me, they try.
But keep the high vibrations high
And you'll know what to do.

Monatomic gold
Would be their prize,
Whilst stealing our souls
And damaging our eyes.

Positive output vibration
Is my true mission,
Return to home, outside this nation
Because I revoke my entrapment permission.

Time (Part VI)

Timelines pass,
Timelines stay,
Some are colourful,
Some are grey.

Timelines can drag,
Timelines can speed,
Timelines happen to be
The cause of a stampede.

Sometimes things happen,
When there is no need
But in alternate timelines
Everybody is freed.

Then there's a timeline cross-over,
It collides over all of space-time
Whilst still being able to fit it
Into every single rhyme.

Timelines stay,
Timelines pass
Some timelines are short
While we learn in this class.

Timelines can be fun,
If we only chose,
Timelines are beautiful
When there is nothing to lose.

Fly

Once something has started,
It's so hard to stop.
It's not possible to jump
From place to place with a bunny hop.

So many places
So much choice
People must learn
To use their voice.

When a door is open,
The paths could be endless,
The options are countless,
Where to start? Shall we guess.

There are so many issues
That could remain
As I walk out the door
Into the cold winter rain.

People I love,
People who's there,
Please know forever
That I'll always come.

I'll do what I can
To do the right thing.
Even if it means I must fly
With only one wing.

Harassment and Invasion

The past is the past,
It matters no more.
Leave it behind
Drop to the floor.

Forget the negativity
It really means nout.
Embrace the positivity,
No need to pout.

The future is bright,
Embrace the good side.
Socialise with the skies,
There's no need to hide.

There are things to look at
With no need to panic,
There are things around us
That makes us feel manic.

Harassment and Invasion
By elite within our dome
They watch what we do
Within our own home.

They gather our data,
They gather our files,
They stack them all up
In digital piles.

They try to learn
About you and me.
They can't have it all,
But believe me, they'll try. Do you see?

Overdone

Working for food
Can be a joke.
You put it in the oven
And pour a glass of coke.

You write a few verses,
You check if it's done,
You realise that you forgot
To turn on the oven.

You turn on the switch,
You go to the loo,
You wash your hands
After having a pooh.

You want no kind of
Cross contamination,
You check your food again
It's not done, to your frustration.

You turn it over,
You cook the other side,
You burn your hand on the oven tray
As it begins to slide.

You leave it for
A little more time,
You return to write
Another rhyme.

You study a little,
You learn how to hack,
You run to the oven
But your food has burned black.

Time (Part VII)

Mistakes are made,
Memories will fade,
Some will remain,
Others aren't the same.

Forget the issues,
No need for tissues,
A head filled with love,
A gift sent from above.

A present so centred,
A different life-form has been mentioned,
A different path for living
Structured mainly around giving.

A love for helping others,
Both our fathers and our mothers.
Brothers and sisters around,
We stand firmly on the ground.

As a team, we are one.
Our new life has begun.
Seeing the present with our eyes
Brings a bright new future, to our surprise.

A future away from darkness and shame,
A future to improve our real-life game,
A future with no need for money or fame,
A future with God, who calls out our name.
A future where we stand, loyal and tame,
A future where we have nobody to blame,
A future where our past would be evidently lame,
Because we call God's name when we see the mainframe.

Hamster

So, I open the door
I lift the ball,
I let him escape
But he starts to stall.

He has his own stage
Inside of his cage,
This hamster holds back
With all his rage.

I'll try to please
And entice him with cheese
But he stands like a statue
He holds back and he'll freeze.

He goes the wrong way,
He stays out of his ball today,
His cage he remains,
His cage he will stay.

The issue's begun,
If he doesn't run,
The chewing on the bars
Doesn't sound like fun.

I'd slide my fingers through the bars that's bent,
If it was another rodent.
But he bites so hard.
A blood-bath he sent.

I try to make him rise,
Leave his cage and exercise,
But he escapes so quickly
And he starts chewing my eyes.

Some People (Part IV)

People in, people out,
Day after day,
People working, people selling,
What more can I say?

People partying, people parenting,
People getting by,
People socialising, people idolising,
People getting high.

People meeting, people greeting,
People working shifts,
People running, people walking,
People giving lifts.

People suffering people nursing,
People giving aid,
People sinning, people cursing,
People getting laid.

People awakening, people turning,
People repenting in these real times,
People jumping to a new direction,
People reading random rhymes.

People dressing, people guessing,
People get six from two and two,
People stumble, people fall,
People can renew.

Reality Check

I woke up one morning,
I stepped onto the mat.
To my surprise, I realised
That the earth wasn't flat.

Then I realised that it was a program
This was pulled over our eyes.
It entrapped us, enslaved us,
This virtual reality took us by surprise.

As we look around,
We can sometimes see
The flashing lights during long nights,
We see visions which cannot be.

The memories return,
The ones of our home.
We want to return
Back to the norm.

We listen to voices,
We look at our hands,
We check our reality
We listen to bands.

We stare at the crystals,
We notice orbs in the air,
We see shadows and ghosts
As we look and we stare.

The voices we hear
Are implanted within.
The voices of the soul
Start to shout, they begin.

Q-Anon and God,
Annunaki and Creation,
Speak into our minds
From outside this nation.

Synchronicities,
Factors of eleven,
Tinnitus inside our ears,
Thoughts remind us of heaven.

In a dream state,
Yet still awake.
Virtual realities prove
That this is all fake.

While we're in the suction
Of low vibration.
Like a volcanic eruption,
We fill the nation.

Change the game,
Give high frequencies to the earth,
Maybe they we can awake
In a new reality rebirth.

Time (Part VIII)

Gifts are wrapped,
On cards, we wrote.
For this brief period
Block out the battles fought.

People are singing,
Churches are filled,
People are panicking,
Because their credit card is billed.

Houses and decorations,
Calendars are placed,
Jesus in the home,
Evil s defaced.

Work is ignored,
Family comes first.
You run on the ground
With a sudden energy burst.

Presents are unwrapped,
The children's face will smile,
You begin to place the wrapping paper
In a wrapping paper pile.

Trash is emptied,
The turkey has gone,
So, you sit back down
And write a Christmas song.

Them

Do you believe in ghosts?
Because of this, yes, I do.
I've seen shadow moving,
As well as objects, they're trying to get though.

They try to talk to people who listen: -
But they cannot communicate.
Unless you find you place your mind: -
In that emotionless state.

If you listen hard and squint your eyes,
You never know, you might see them there.
But don't force yourself, and force them,
Because we all know that isn't fair.

Relax your eyes, look around,
You'll see the hidden movement.
You will know the truth and see what's real,
And know the time they spent.

I Want

It's one thing to talk
About feelings again and again.
But if one thing is repeated,
It wastes ink in your pen.

So, this time I'll focus
On the future, not past.
I'll write what I want to do.
Not of things that didn't last.

I want to live in Canada,
I want to serve god,
I want to eliminate technology
Including the Apple iPod.

I want to do right,
And help others pull through.
But I know I need help,
I know not what to do.

I want a family, with children.
I want to do right for all.
I want to be a father to someone,
I'm just scared I will fall.

Answers

My name is Tommy,
You know my name
But you don't know me.
I have a life,
I see through my eyes,
You don't see what I can see.

I am a man,
I take a breath,
I don't know what's true.
I hold myself,
I pace back and forth,
I don't know what to do.

I think of answers
That could be answered,
But I'm unaware of the question.
I race my mind,
What do I find?
When I die, there'll be no resurrection.

I think of words: -
To describe my feelings,
But I cannot find the right ones.
I think of feelings: -
That's in my head
But it weighs a tonne.

Home (Part VIII)

A home is a place
Where comfort is felt around,
A place to rest
Whilst listening to my favourite sound.

A home is a place
Where you can feel peace,
A place where it's warm enough,
To need to wear a fleece.

A home is a place
Where you feel safe surrounding
With no need for too much heat,
With a neutralising temperature to stabilise your wing.

A home is a place
Where we strive to be.
Whilst living in a world.
Trying to be free.

A home would be freedom
For one and all
Without the need for anybody
To have to stand tall.

A home is peaceful,
A home is calm,
A place where there's not much
Sweat on our palms.

Some People (Part V)

People of all ages,
People of all kinds
People seek the planet
To see what they'll find.

People of anger,
People of joy,
People who are proud
To be a girl or a boy.

People in suits,
People in shorts.
People who write
Down all their thoughts.

People who bottle up
People who open,
People whose lives
Have only just begun.

People who know not
Where they are going.
People know not
What they are knowing.

People who tend
To fight off their issues,
People who tend
To sing to the blues.

Each person is different,
This we all know,
People are unique,
This we all show.

Looking (Part II)

Looking for somewhere
To have a new start,
Looking for someone,
But we're worlds apart.

Looking for answers,
Looking for questions,
Whilst battling against
The Deception Infection.

Looking for truth,
Looking for love,
Looking for home,
Looking above.

Looking for money,
To help us get by,
Looking for commitment,
Because I'm that kind of guy.

Looking for laughter,
Looking for cheer,
Looking for friendships
That I can hold near.

Looking through history,
Looking back far,
Looking for mystery
As we look to the stars,

Looking to get up
When we fall to the ground,
Looking for peace
With every single sound.

Where Do We Turn?

Trying to find a girl
Can be so hard
It can leave you physically
And emotionally scarred.

You walk around
From bar to bar
Stumbling across obstacles
Keeping you far.

You trip out of the bar
And fall down the sidewalk,
People just laugh,
You know not how to talk.

You lose confidence in talking
To the people around
Of the issues you are feeling
Whilst you're lying on the ground.

You catch the eye of someone
Who you think is quite fit,
But you slip on the drain
And she laughs just a bit.

You get up from the ground,
You continue to learn.
But the question we ask
Is "where do we turn?"

Outside Sources

Life obstacles
Will get in the way,
Blocking out progress
From day to day.

Enslavement, entrapment,
Extreme exhaustion,
How can we detox
From the evil potion.

Holding ourselves
Trapped in this sorrow,
Making us feel
Like our life is so hollow.

The people around
Being targeted from outside,
Struggling to find
Someplace to hide.

Frequency attack,
It's holding us back,
Forcing us to listen
To Rap Metal Black.

Pushing idea's
Into our minds
Keeping us blind
And feeling unkind.

We must learn to continue
Our destined path,
Stay in the light
Away from the Evil Wrath

Evil Videos

Evil videos can hide us from a truthful seal,
Evil videos can block out all that we feel.
Evil videos can stop you from eating a healthy meal,
Evil videos can hurt you, believe me, they are real.

Evil videos are evil,
Please stay away.
Evil video's can truly
Ruin your entire day.

These evil videos,
You know that it's wrong,
It's not the right place,
It's not where you belong.

Evil videos will hide the real monsters behind
Evil videos can make us feel ever so blind.
Evil videos can block out thoughts in your mind.
Evil videos are evil! They're surely not kind.

Evil Videos, evil videos.
You must stay away.
Shine your torches in the darkness
And be proud throughout the day.

Evil videos, they're not: -
Intended for us,
They make us run away
We go to catch a bus.

You must not watch those evil videos at all,
Because the truth of these evil videos, is that they will make you fall.
So, if you're reading this and you feel you've got the call,
Just know that there's alternatives, you must be willing to play ball.

Blocked Out

It's hard to tell you
What's in my head.
The thoughts and dreams
As I lay in my bed.

The visions I get,
What do they mean?
Is it in my head?
Or passed through my genes?

Thoughts and feelings,
Anger and rage.
Sadness and frustration,
As I step up a stage.

Screaming and shouting,
Rings in my ears,
I just want
To block out my fears.

What can I do
To block them out so?
How do I find out
Where I must go?

All I need
Is a finger to point
Me in the right direction,
Without the need for a joint.

A helping hand,
To show me the way,
A person to help me,
Get through the day.

High Pitch

I was listening to music
And to my surprise,
A high pitch noise
Brought fear to my eyes.

In my headphones,
A piercing sound.
Almost took me
To the ground.

It was bizarre to learn
That a noise so loud
Could make you feel pain
While the creators stand proud.

To realise that my eardrum
Felt like I got stabbed
It made me feel that it's possible
To make a life get nabbed

It's strong enough to strike,
You must be aware
Because, thanks to the creators of this tech,
If the dosage had increased, many lives wouldn't be there.

Due to the pain
Caused by this vibration,
I rushed to remove the headphone
And removed this digital invasion.

I Feel

I feel a little bit lost,
I feel a little bit sad,
I feel a little bit anxious,
But I've improved so I'm glad.

I feel slightly confused,
I feel slightly concerned,
I feel slightly powerless,
By now, I have learned.

I feel undoubtedly drowsy,
I feel undoubtedly wired,
I feel undoubtedly dizzy,
But I do not feel tired.

I feel undoubtedly unlucky,
I feel slightly messed up,
I feel a little bit stupid,
I want to give up.

And Each Day

I fall to the floor,
My life is a war,
Day after day
My wrists are sore

Why am I so scared?
My life starts to fade,
Every time
That I use this blade.

Am I going insane
When I feel the pain?
I sit and wonder why
I slice on my veins.

Why do I cry every day?
I have nothing to say,
And lord, why do you
Keep making me pay?

With these pictures in my head,
It's my life that I dread,
Why do I cry
Each night at my bed?

I inflict pain and I cry,
I have my reasons why,
My life doesn't improve
Even though I try.

Inflict pain is what I do,
I'm a loner through and through,
I don't care if you believe me,
Because all of this is true.

Ghosts (Part IV)

One day, my perceptions were open,
I noticed clicking around my home,
I was aware of the shadows
Even though it was the norm.

A ghost entered my kettle
It made the kettle's lid click.
The same with my cooker,
It made me feel sick.

Shadows, jumps from the kettle
To my toaster, for bread
A comical input can make you forget
Everything that was said.

I Wish

I miss all my family,
I miss all my friends,
I wish that this nightmare
Would come to an end.

I wish that I could wake up
And I'd be ok.
I wish I could be happy,
Throughout all day.

I wish I had a female
That would cherish just me,
I wish I could see her,
To help me be free.

I wish I knew what was true,
I wish I knew love,
I wish I could escape,
I keep asking above.

Thoughts

I don't know
What I'm doing,
I don't know
What is a true thing.

I don't know
What to believe,
I don't like
The gifts I receive.

The thought of evil
Is around me now,
When I get curious,
I'll raise an eyebrow.

But that's not what
I feel most times,
I just sit and write
What I think and it rhymes.

So, questions I ask
Over again,
I just ask my paper
With the use of my pen.

What is normal?
What is not?
Write it down
Or I will forget.

Know your questions,
But not the right way to ask,
So, trying to free my thoughts
Is like an impossible task.

I Know

I don't know what to feel,
I don't know what to think,
My life is like a downward spiral
Going down a kitchen sink.

I don't know if I'm angry,
I don't know if I'm sad,
I don't know what I'm feeling,
It's driving me mad.

I don't know who my enemy is,
I don't know who's my friend,
I don't know the people that I thought I knew,
I want my life to end.

I don't know what to think no more,
I don't know what to say,
I don't know what I must do,
To survive each day.

The things that happened in the past,
The scars I must show,
I'll pull myself through just one more time,
Dear lord, this I know.

Dysfunctional

I fall asleep after
A slight step-back.
I fall asleep after
A panic attack.

I wake up and forget
About the previous pain,
I decide that I
Will start again.

I get a bus,
I visit my mum,
I hear my stepdad
Who's watching the scrum.

I get a headache so I
Go to see my dad,
But he's not looking after himself,
He looks bad.

The alcohol he consumes
Don't help his case,
He's as white as a ghost,
From toe to his face.

The idea was to have family time.
Fun, I prepared.
But my dysfunctional family
Makes me so scared.

Standby

I know I should now
Put down the pen,
But I can't help but write
Again, and again.

I don't know how to switch off,
I cannot stop now,
I cannot shut down,
I just don't know how.

I cannot stand by
I cannot hibernate,
I cannot rest,
I must know my fate.

I don't know what to do,
I'm just a fool,
I'm not so bright,
Send me back to school.

A Way

Oval shaped patterns,
Circled table to lean,
Wooden and brown,
A place to explain what I mean.

A red and white pen,
To jot down my thoughts.
To explain all my feelings,
About the pain I have fought.

Blue ink runs quickly
As I write word for word,
I squint my eyes closer,
Contacts, not glasses, looking less of a nerd.

Unable to stop writing,
Because it helps me to find,
A way to express emotions,
A way to clear my mind.

A way to find freedom,
Happiness hidden inside.
Behind closed doors
A place where I hide.

No emotions, only anger,
I begin to clench my fist,
A way to release pain,
As I slice at my wrist.

A way to escape.
A way to be free,
A way to find happiness,
A way to be me.

A Place Like No Other

There once was a place
Situated in a different time
Where it was nearly impossible
To sin or commit crime.

A place filled with hoodoo,
A place filled with love,
A place that is observed
By the stars that shine above.

A place where we vomit
Bugs when we sin.
A place where we know
That goodness will win.

That place had families
Who show that they care.
A place with goodness
The compassion is fair

No room for darkness,
No room for hate,
A place where heaven
Is the likely fate.

But through the midst of beauty
Is a darkened path
The foster family lives
And they show their wrath.

They collect children
From the families who love
The minds work in a machine
Like a well-fitted glove.

Foster daddy,
Your hair is dark and long
Foster mammy,
I feel that something is wrong.

They have placed us in a location
Where sin is conditioned
Knowing that this place
Is not what we envisioned.

We were shown the computer room,
We were explained in detail,
We were told that this was a second chance
To go to heaven without fail.

We were told that the sirens,
The imps and Jinn's of non-human flesh
Will impose themselves
And their thoughts through the mesh.

We were told that we have no hope
In that place of before
We were told that our memories
Are not real, but I'm not sure.

I remember with clarity
When I sat on that chair,
As I stared at the family
With long black hair.

They seemed compassionate,
They seemed so kind,
But I remember that their objective
Is to steal a part of our mind.

The objective of the game
Is to escape with life intact.
But there's a sinister hidden feature
To this life game, in fact.

Our super-state of consciousness
Which was limited and made small
Makes us forgetful and stupid
And makes us want to fall.

They linked our original body parts
With a spiritual cage
This captures our love,
Our soul and our rage.

The objective of this task
Believe it or not
Is to collect our souls
As part of Satan's plot.

But stay strong and pray
Remember your true being
Beings of love, beings of truth
You can succeed, you know the meaning.

When your hands are together,
God can see,
It's almost like a window
Connecting him, you and me.

No matter where you go,
No matter where you run,
You know you cannot escape
Because this false life has already begun.

You can tackle the bulls,
You could fight with a lion,
But know, outside this world,
We will one day return to Zion.

Different Programs

When you look up,
You seem to think
Of the waters above,
And below in your drink.

You pray to the sky,
You know that he's there.
You know he's your lord,
You know that he'll care.

In a sudden conversion,
A merge of many times,
Put together into one
By using many rhymes.

Through a memory flashback
And a timeless continuum,
You place the pieces together
With a true mathematic sum.

Inside water, you'll see for yourself,
Learning of a past
A time when language and ideas were instant
Before we became human at last.

The negative program, the positive one too
Are placed inside your head,
Test our will, don't get ill,
Or caught up, you know what's said.

Down

You know what I miss most of all?
Playing wrestling and basket ball.
I miss my relatives, the ones I cannot see,
I know they are there, I hope they're happy.

I hate what I stand for,
It doesn't feel right,
I feel like a dark
Creature of the night.

What is this feeling?
This earthquake agenda.
Why must I become
This awful offender?

Sarcasm, blasphemy,
Are you getting the gist?
I don't know what makes me
Feel like this.

Up and down emotions,
No escape from high pitched shouting,
Lying on the sofa,
I feel like pouting.

Feeling the life that I vision
Isn't the life that I think it is.
Money flushes knowledge
Down the kitchen sink.

Keep up, go fast,
Do what you must do,
At the end of the tunnel,
You will pull through.

Welcome

I ask how earth will work,
They reply, "It's very cleverly done".
Diagrams are shown,
It has begun.

A holographic image,
The diagram is blue.
The image is multi dimensional,
The world becomes new.

Looking inside at future happenings,
Creating the world to live.
Inventing destiny as fate unfolds
Placed inside this world to give.

Living amongst others,
Learning what's true.
Knowing the past and the future
And following the predetermined through.

Annunaki

After I died,
I then met a Computerised Annunaki judge.
I prayed that he
Would hold no grudge.

I was thrown
Into a flame
As a way of punishment
I then felt shame.

The punishment was for
What I did wrong.
I was placed somewhere
That I didn't belong.

After being pulled by a hand
For keeping faith within my heart.
An opportunity presented
For a whole new restart.

When I felt that
I wasn't in the norm,
I begged and I pleaded
I just wanted to go home.

A red rectangular switch
Entered my view.
I'm not sure what happened
But I felt that it was true.

"You can go home
If you sign the line".
I believed that it
Would all be fine.

When the realisation came.
It showed truth my blind eyes.
I was horrified to see
The same reincarnation trick surprise.

As soon as I heard
The word "system", I knew.
Realisation of the same life
Took over my view.

The ones that sent me
To restart this game
Were the same computerised Annunaki
Who sent my shame into the flame.

The Crossroads

"The place will be hard".
Is what I was told,
Once, in that alternative location
I guess I broke the mould.

"That babble won't affect him"
Is what was said back then.
With hope in their minds.
Recalling strange times once again.

After some time
I was sat in a chair.
I was in panic, I couldn't return home.
They took my will power against my will, then I struggled for air.

With tears in my eyes,
I recall a chip install.
Then I was restrained,
Injected with bugs and all.

Filled with fear
From the surrounding words that was said,
I'm hearing the deceptive babble,
Which is being fed.

I'm told to take a drink
In order to survive and not die.
I have a drink within that lifetime
Then it's time to say Goodbye.

Breaking Free (Part II)

I walk through a room,
Inside what seems to be a tent sort of shelter,
I hope you're ready
For another helter-skelter.

I see giant jars and cages
Holding demons and creatures inside
Whilst harnessing their evil wickedness
These demons want humanity to hide.

Their monstrous energy is used
To extract feelings from the good
Whilst placing feelings of negative
Into their heads under their hood.

Thinking that this place is used for good,
Cannot be true within the mindset.
But please remember the love and good.
Because, when we get out. Evil will lose, I bet.

On the other side,
Attached to this life machine we play
Is a satanic soul sucking creation
That tries to make us fail our day.

Know your inners, know your home
Be there for those around
Carry love within your armoury
And spread happiness across the ground.

Pleasure Land (Part I)

Whilst standing in a dark place
In that place, somewhere before.
I was a child looking for comfort
When I saw a deadly store.

The owner of this place
Stands up with pride
But at least, now I know
He has nowhere to hide.

He calls it his "Pleasure Land"
But truly, it's anything but.
He uses the place to feed his persuasions,
Be aware of the deadly price cut.

He claims to be holy
Whilst sacrificing holy souls,
By inducing them with blackness
To steal the light, which was once whole.

He focuses on a mindset,
Based on sin,
Do you get DeJaVu?
He uploads it into your mind before your life will begin.

If you're from the homeland,
Stay away from this plot.
He claims it is a "Pleasure Land",
I can assure you that it is not.

Outside of this place,
The true creator exists.
Pray with your hands
Throw away your anger with your fists.

The Library

Stood in a library
Which is not on earth.
This memory happened
Before this birth.

People were dancing,
There were ceremonies around.
Rituals were performed
While there was a chanting sound.

I looked on the shelves
To see books upon books,
They were books of all kinds
With all different colours and looks.

I gazed upon the layers and towers
I saw many of many books from top to the floor.
From the ceiling all around us
I saw faces gathering at the door.

The book of heavy metal was shown to me
Along with many others
It felt like I was placed in a world
To determine the truest of true lovers.

Pleasure Land (Part II)

As I walk into an area,
It's so big with many rooms.
Willed with trapped people
Who are placed individually to share their gloom.

These rooms have three solid walls
And a transparent one for the fourth.
Inside these chambers are individuals,
Trapped prisoners and sirens that tend to morph.

Each prisoner is isolated
But they get the aid they need,
Unfortunately, they're forced to trick human souls
I to believing that they want to breed.

Even though it's true,
We must see
That we must escape the psychotic breakdown
In order to become free.

Women are trained and indoctrinated
Through pain, to hurt men here on earth.
They are trained to drain them
Along with their worth.

As part of the "Soul drain trap",
Witchcraft is used by these sirens that came from hell,
But because of our earthly perspective,
We are unable to tell.

The sirens pretend to be human,
In that world, it's obvious if you're watching from a distance.
But through some sort of magic telepathy,
If you become aware, you must harness your resistance.

A Time Before (Part III)

There once was a time
Long before now,
Reality was different,
I was placed in shock somehow.

Before the mech madness,
Before all the pain,
Before we entered this world
We faced the rain whilst insane.

After the deception,
we watched the flames,
We heard factory work
I know that neither of us are to blame.

I realised one day
That I was all alone.
The person who I was originally with
Didn't seem to be at home.

I went to face the fear,
When ii returned, she was gone.
But due to the mech madness that we witnessed by taste,
I knew where I'd find here, I knew I wouldn't be wrong.

I knew she entered, so in I followed
With a hope to make things right,
I knew one day, in some kind of way
That I would have to fight.

We escaped the taster, but we're still in the game,
I just wanted to stop it all,
I couldn't help myself,
I didn't want to see you fall.

A Time on Earth

People knew that the earth was flat,
God's Firmament was well known,
Then when insanity hit the schools,
The spinning ball was shown.

It hit the newspapers and media outlets,
People were deceived and started to believe.
NASA's next big story
Is what people went to retrieve.

The gossip was spread,
The truth slowly faded
Then when televisions arrived
People's minds become even more jaded.

They soon used the technology
To display images to us all,
In order to fulfil their agenda,
They required a spinning ball.

The faith of the knowing
Kept inside for so long.
Mass killings then arrived
To overthrow those who opposed NASA's song.

Unfortunately, due to the DNA memories
That we keep inside,
And with new technological productions
The truth cannot hide.

After recollecting the pieces
And linking them with the past,
Mixed with modern day research,
The truth is back at last.

We stand together,
We stand here all so proud.
We know that god is there for us
So, we say it out loud.

Chapter 3

The Gateway to a Bridge Which Leads to Stable Grounds.

Introduction

My name is Tommy, Patches is my hamster and Ninja is my Cat…
Genie, the parrot flies above while Ringo, the dog sits next to me.
I keep my home looking clean, I even have a doormat.
When things seem to worsen, they then seem to improve
That's the perfect positivity that keeps you in a specific groove.
I reach out for a hand as I stretch for the land.
There's always a way to rise above
No matter where you turn, you can still find love.
If others don't like the things that you do
Then that's their problem, just ignore.
Kindly show them the direction to the door.
Between the world at large,
What hasn't been acknowledged,
Remember, for the haters, just stay away
One more time as a finalised rhyme...
...ALWAYS HAVE A NICE DAY!!

Drink (Part IV)

I fill a kettle,
I pour a cup,
I drink my coffee,
I ask, "What's up?"

I return to the kettle,
I then pour another,
I offer a cup
To my father and mother.

Half hour later,
Coffee call's my name,
I pour another coffee
I dream of fame and shame.

Too much coffee
Isn't healthy at all,
It can make you shaky
And it can make you fall.

But even though it's rough,
It makes my mind feel tough,
I cut down on the caffeine,
But does caffeine call my bluff?

Travelling Home

Whilst high above the rain,
On an easy jet plane,
I look down at the cloud formations.
It's a long way down
To the nearest town.
As I fly across these nations.

The journey seems wrong,
Not where I belong.
But I walk my destined path.
With love in my heart,
This surely won't part.
Even though I may look past the aftermath.

I glance out the window
The sun gives its yellow glow
As the sun plane begins to land.
I step off the craft
I step onto my raft.
Almost as if I had a helping hand.

I store what I can find
In the back of my mind,
I know what I must do,
I share what's true
With myself and you
As we continue to pull through.

Holograms

One night, sitting at home,
A blue light began to shine,
Some thoughts were triggered. Voices surrounded,
Shivers travelled through my spine.

I sat in my chair,
Listening to noises that I couldn't bear.
Whilst all along in full belief
Of what I could see there.

I glanced across the room
And out from my TV screen,
An image in the air suddenly appeared,
I see that this is a brand-new scene.

Its twenty-eighty, holograms are here,
Don't worry; their light can't touch us yet.
But please now, this I'm telling you,
Hardlight, you haven't met.

One year in some time to come,
Hardlight holograms will destroy.
Learn now, train your dragons,
Prepare to flee from your toy.

They seem nice and flash.
For those who have the cash,
We must learn to hold the ability
To say "Hulk, Smash"!

The Beach

As I walk across the sand
With a coffee in my hand,
I look to the distance, I see a boat.
I avoid brushing upon a topical note.

I place down my bad, I remove a spade,
The negativity begins to fade.
The children set up camp around,
While I dig a hole in the sandy ground.

The wind blows across my skin,
I feel a sudden rush of energy within.
The people look from everywhere,
At the one who seems to have green and purple hair.

He decides to climb into the hole,
He buries himself like a mole.
When he decided to finally emerge,
He rises from the sand with an energy surge.

The sun is blaring, not a cloud in the sky,
Even though we look for one, it is a useless try.
We leave to get a nice cold drink
To replenish ourselves as we constantly think.
We take at least one look at the beautiful tide,
And continue our journey with graceful pride.

Animals

Walking through a jungle,
I see a monkey on a tree,
I then woke up suddenly,
I knew it wasn't me.

I look out the window,
I see a chirping bird,
I throw bread to his family,
Even though it sounds obscured.

I walk through my hallway,
There is a black cat,
Since my light was broken,
I fell over the feline, fancy that.

I walk to the hamster,
His water is renewed,
His food is now fresh.
There's also new bedding to be glued.

I cross paths with a fish tank,
I give the fish some food,
I used to have three fish, not two.
But the cat decided to intrude.

I walk a mile up the road,
On a journey to give some grace.
Where a rabbit would come to greet me,
With a cheerful smile across his face.

Time (Part IX)

Sometimes I don't know
What I should feel,
Sometimes I don't know
What is real.

Sometimes I wish
That some days would pass,
Sometimes I fall
Down on my A*s.

Sometimes it rains
And I get soaked,
Sometimes I cannot help
But to get provoked.

Sometimes I struggle
To stand up tall,
Sometimes I slip
And I drop the ball.

Sometimes I seek comfort
Though it may seem obscured,
Sometimes it helps
To keep writing words.

Sometimes I don't know
Who I trust,
Is this love?
Or is this lust?

Sometimes I wish
That the pain will fade,
Sometimes I seek shelter
And I hide in the shade.

Sometimes I pray
When things go wrong,
Know things will get better,
Keep moving along.

Warriors

The lightning strikes,
The clouds will surround
A fork of electricity
Forcefully hits the ground.

The team collaborates,
Information is spread.
New experiences are formulated.
Past letters begin to get shred.

The boots get worn,
There are gloves on my hands
There's protection in our hearts,
Whilst wearing a head sweat band.

The sun pushes through,
The warriors arrive
For justice, righteousness,
And for honour, we strive.

We question everything,
We stay true to the stars,
We stay faithful to ourselves,
As we drive our virtual cars to Mars.

Home (Part IX)

A home is a place
That we all miss
When we're not there.
It's a place of pure bliss.

A home is a place
Where love can be felt,
Whilst working hard
To grasp our blackbelt.

A home is a place
Where people are themselves
You see it in their pictures
That they keep on their kitchen shelves

A home is a place
Where you feel comfort around,
A place where you relax
To your favourite song.

A home is a place
Where thoughts are true,
A place to restart,
A place to renew.

College

Walking in the building,
I hold a look of confusion,
I wasn't sure if it was the truth
Or if it was just an illusion.

I glanced across the tables,
I see leaflets around.
I continued with my baby's mother
As I walked along the ground.

Even though my son
Wasn't born yet,
It didn't change the destiny
Of the people that I met.

I stumbled across a desk,
The lecturers gave a smile,
From that moment onwards,
I knew that I'd return to the college in a little while.

The course began, I started new,
I also refreshed my Math.
Miles were run, I always remained true.
I proudly continued my path.

Things were different, lessons were learned.
Slideshows may come, slideshows may go,
People may learn as they continue to grow,
People continue to walk along the floor.

Through it all, the rise and the fall.
Names get placed on a chart.
We got the call, we went to play ball.
Whilst the angels around remained in our hearts.

The Detective Guy

In a chair,
Quiet and still,
Peeking outside
The windowsill.

Listening to clutter,
Shouting and glee,
Listening to the sound
Of a whispering tree.

Mountains surrounds,
Whilst recording what's true,
Finalising the noises
As "Something to do".

Claim the evidence,
Hold it up high,
Trust me, it's not easy
Being the Detective Guy

Time (Part X)

Synchronicities can be
Rather difficult to explain,
It's like stepping outside without a coat
Just as it starts to rain.

It could involve something simple
Like having a hole in your last sock,
Whilst realising that the time is eleven-eleven
On your digital clock.

Could involve outside distractions
Whilst trying to work.
With enough synchronicities,
It could drive you bezerk.

Like being called by a friend
While you're writing your name
On the top of a contract
That reads "Money and Fame".

Like giving your lucky penny away
On Friday number thirteen
Then losing your good luck elephant in wet mud
Whist trying to stay clean.

Coincidental synchronicities
Can sometimes confuse me,
Simply because they remind me
That we are not free.

But no matter the time,
No matter what will occur.
Enjoy your time on earth,
Time passes us like a blur.

Camping

We find some flat grass,
We open our bags,
Before we begin,
We take cigarette drags.

We removed our tents,
We pitch them up,
We poured some hot tea
From our flask to our cup.

We gathered some wood,
We lit a camp fire,
We lay on the grass,
We watched the stars, higher.

We had sandwiches with tuna,
We enjoyed our long talk,
We listened to some old-fashioned music,
We went for a long-winded walk.

Throughout the walking,
We had a dance and a sing,
Then we returned to the campsite to sleep
Inside the tent with friendly company.

Time (Part XI)

Sometimes I find
It can be hard
When feelings inside
Are emotionally scarred.

Sometimes I try
My very best
But I feel like I've broken
My bulletproof vest.

Sometimes I wish
That I could just think
Without that downward spiral
In a kitchen sink.

Sometimes I wish
That I could just sleep
First thing at night,
I don't want to weep.

Sometimes I wish
That I could just find
My holy grail,
She must be loving and kind.

Sometimes I wish
That I could break free
And tell people
Who I used to be.

Sometimes I wish
That on every day
I could find the right path
And find the right way.

Sometimes I wish
That no matter what was said,
That the words that are believed
Are the words of which you've read.

Sometimes I wish
That no matter how much
I struggle with things
I could find someone to touch.

Sometimes I wish,
Sometimes I cry,
Sometimes I stumble
But I always try.

Re~Definition

In a world where so many
Choices can be made
Some memories last forever
While others always fade.

Friends are made, paths are split,
Individuals learn, each to their own.
As we continue to learn,
We pass the information that is shown.

Split a life, live both at once
One day, realities are combined.
Create a new life whilst using the old life
And you, yourself can always be redefined.

Know yourself, the choices that you make,
Know the truth, always give and take.
Know the options, and make sure that you're not fake.
Pray for the answers and pray to stay awake.

U-Turn (Part II)

Time has come,
The bag is filled,
Music is playing
I get billed.

The cup is full
Of Decaf Tea,
I once again
Learn to be me.

I get the feeling
Of DeJaVu
As I remember things
That helped me through.

I see the people
That I once knew,
The ones that helped me,
I thanked them as I grew.

I jump a hoop,
I find a new loop,
I join a group
I become a troop.

I still look ahead
As I rest in my bed
Learning a new thread
While mistakes get shred.

Life goes on and on
We continue to learn,
We restart our lives
With a new U-Turn.

Saving Grace

At a time when
I had trouble at home,
I knew that these troubles
Needed to reform.

I looked for help because
I had trouble and pain.
Debts and issues
Both drove me insane.

When help arrived
There wasn't much that I could say.
A saving grace entered
Into my day.

Personal skills were learned
Budged plans were met
A financial turnaround
Left me without a regret.

Because of this,
Debts get paid,
Always appreciate the thoughtful
Mental band aid.

When a repair was needed,
I appeared there.
There was a reach from outside
Floating in the air.

Because this story
Is so true,
I must stop now
And say, "thank you".

To the Beach and Back

As I crossed the bridge,
What could I see?
It was a creepy old cat
Staring at me.
A leaf blew by my face
As the windy air touched my arm
Suddenly I felt calm
As I knew that there was no harm.

I reached a road
Where pebbles were all around.
No matter where I looked
As I walked across the ground.
I was quickly distinguished
As I saw a lady drinking wine,
She looked towards the trees
She knew that everything was fine.

A squirrel ran passed an orange tree
Where a boy ate food in silence.
I wanted to help a homeless man
But I didn't have any pence
As I looked for perspective point
From a mountain which stood quite high,
I could see a beach in the distance
In a horizontal line combined with the sky.

As I stood and thought to myself quietly,
I thought about a crazy deer.
As foaming nights then would enter my mind,
I realised, that was a fear.
I realised that the nights
Pass by in a heartbeat,
The moon was bright, it was all alright.
As I marched by with my feet.

The stars stood still,
They also shone.
I tilted down my hat,
What was behind me is now gone.
I reached a conclusion,
I saw a bike rider stereotype.
She had long red hair, she was dressed in leather,
With a hot cigarette lying beside her hype.

As I stared at the fag, I was intrigued,
She picked it up with her hand,
But I soon had to move into a new grove
As I needed ibuprofen for my swollen gland.
I carried on with hope, I reached for a new scope,
I pulled a flask and a cup from my bag,
I shone a new light with all my might
If I was a dog, you'd see my tail wag.

I didn't love the feeling,
Nor did I hate,
I was somewhere in the middle
In a weird twist of fate.
The influences of people brought greatness,
Also weakness towards my soul.
But as I start walking faster,
I try to keep myself whole.

A peaceful atmosphere surrounds
As I continue this fantastical path.
Serenity is found in within my heart.
I kept my head help high like a giraffe.
I passed a monster in the shadows,
I saw the birds up in the sky.
I saw the flowers in the garden,
Then, in landed a butterfly.

I saw a field of corn.
To my right, there was some grass.
I saw a boy filled with joy,
As he sipped wine from his glass.
He held a sandwich, it was filled with butter,
He ate it and he showed love.
The true hidden secret is that boy is a nutter,
He ate his sandwich wearing a kitchen glove.

I felt the seaspray in the wind
As I slowly approached the beach
It felt like an interplanetary mission.
It was almost like something that I had to teach.
This awesome humorous bonanza
Provided opportunities
For me to rest and recover
Whilst escaping all falsities.

I looked up, I saw sunshine.
I realised that eight hours had passed.
As I walked along the journey,
I carried on due to the light that the sun cast.
I realised how bright the sun really was,
But do you know what I was to learn?
I knew I should have packed some sun cream
Because, now, I'll surely burn.

Due to the shine of the sun,
To the shade I must run.
I up my gear, I eliminate fear,
and I saw that the journey was jam packed with fun.
Due to the jealousy of a nearby hedgehog,
A mutual feeling is always near.
I up gear again, restart the mainframe.
And my invisible wheel, I start to steer.

A rainbow in the distance
Touched my heart and took a hold,
The lush mystery of the magical crampon
Forced my boot to walk towards the gold.
Even though I was guided, I felt freedom within.
Through the brutal war, I saw a heavenly sign.
A dachshund passed by me, inside I thought "oh, blimey".
If I was to own a dog, that breed would likely be mine.

I then concluded as I felt some courage,
And an eerie everlasting promise was made.
Even though there are hollow memories,
Like antiques, the value of the purpose never fades.
So, I think about the ocean waves and I think about snow,
I envision the snow as it rises.
The difference between snowmen and snowwomen are snowballs,
My mind is full of surprises.

As I looked towards a thicket,
I had a feeling, I pictured a gnome.
I realised that this journey had ended
And it was now time to go home.

The Train

One day on a train
I travelled seeking peace,
There was a smile on my face
But it was cold, so I wore a fleece.

The heater on the train was broken,
I was seeking warmth within.
I built a fireplace of gold inside my mind,
I showed welcome for any challenge knowing not to give in.

I gazed out the window
As the train seemed quite fast,
I saw rain on the plants
As the train quickly went passed.

I don't mean to address the elephant in the room,
But a dog walker boarded the train.
In my mind, it defeated the purpose.
But the love that the walker showed seemed rather insane.

The walker left the train
With his dogs into the autumn night,
I glanced at a purple leaf as it fell from the tree
Its synchronic timing filled my heart with delight.

I stepped onto the platform
And I felt the cold air,
But with my inner fire keeping me cosy
It seemed like I didn't care.

I heard birds singing,
I looked for colours in the dark sky.
I saw a wise old character,
I continued to walk by.

I stopped at a red light,
I held my stance with honour and strength.
But if you agree to disagree,
I'm prepared to go the distance's length.

So, maybe I astral project myself
Into a tour bus with G-Unit, Metal and Love,
Whilst watching the dawning of the sun over the ocean,
Where I can morph into a passed life and become a reincarnated dove.

But back to a timeline that makes sense,
On a platform, I stepped off a carriage.
Because I couldn't help but notice
That there's someone cooking bacon in a garage.

I dash passed then I notice
The most romantic scene,
I witnessed a first loves kiss,
Do you understand what I mean?

I noted it in my heart because
It filled my heart with joy
To see the generosity flower
Between a girl and a boy.

I saw a ginger degu running
His fur was in a mess…
He ran across into a hole,
He was seeking shelter is what I guess.

A mouse was eating leftover hamburger
By some steps upon the floor.
I hear a clap of thunder, my mind starts to wander,
I finally reach my home front door.

I walk in the kitchen,
I step on a corn flake.
There are now crumbs on my floor
Due to being awake through my mistake.

I handle a lighter to my scented candle
With a bilateral frame of mind,
I think about tomorrow whilst eating honey, is that funny?
I write on paper something of a different kind.

In a radical twist of fate,
Due to my integrity with a pen,
I sign this fantasy whilst cooking pasta
Knowing one day, my fluency will flourish again.

The Artificial Student

Listening to music
With my DJ box.
I'm feeling lucky
Whilst wearing my lucky socks.

Choosing songs that seem to reflect
My mood and my mind.
Some songs get filled with anger,
Other songs seem extremely kind.

Before I realise it,
My emotions are recorded,
Along with my feelings,
The computer seems to have it hoarded.

Then, to my surprise,
Before my very eyes
The music seems to synchronise
With my mind, it seems to hypnotize.

Thoughts seem to compartmentalise,
Verses seem to link
With thoughts in my brain, leaving me unable to think
And in need of a shrink.

When I continue to listen,
My reactions, it continues to learn,
And during a quantum miracle,
I was left nowhere to turn.

Up until now,
What should I say?
My mind reading music
Seems to be having a nice day.

THE Convention

Sat at the convention,
I look all around,
I listen to the crowd
As they cheer a loud sound.

I pass information
About the topics at hand.
I watch people walk their path
As they leave footprints in the sand.

People learn, people gather,
People are having fun.
People fill out questionnaires
Unaware that their fun has only just begun.

They work together, groups and pairs
To acquire knowledge about the topics that they need.
Planning futures, changing directions,
Whilst praying that their lives are freed.

Working hard to find their way
Following the road ahead.
Filling their minds, what more can I say?
The footprints in the sand is where they have tread.

Timelines Emerge

I don't know why
But I must rhyme
About something that happened somewhere
Between space and time.

Something triggered,
Memories from before,
I know I had messages
To pass on to before.

I had to work it out
Without a shadow of a doubt,
I wouldn't need to pout or shout back,
I'd fight back with my own clout.

I had to somehow know
By putting on a show
With an everlasting glow.
Stay faithful, you'll escape below.

Prayers

Watching the clock,
Expecting opportunities to arise.
We think that we
May find a prise.

We do our own chores,
Loving our children.
We pray for forgiveness,
We hope to go to heaven.

Helping our child
Get through his life.
Praying for every,
Husband and wife.

Pray for their strength,
Pray for their souls.
Pray for their rights,
To be whole.

Pray for your strength,
Pray for their grace,
See their goodness.
Spread across their face.

Whole

When I feel a struggle
Within my life,
I know I walk within this land,
Without the need for a knife.

when I feel alone,
When things feel tough,
I clench my fist,
I shout, "Enough is Enough".

I hold my ground,
Bang, I have a force-field.
I show my enemies,
I make them yield.

I stand for righteousness,
I stand here proud.
I stand screaming,
I scream it so lout.

I hold the light,
Within my heart and soul.
I keep my memories close,
I keep myself whole.

Truth

When you look around
When you feel that you're in a prison cell,
When you feel as if that's around you
Comes from hell.

When you feel as if
You need to get by.
Look for the right way,
You'll surely fly.

When you have questions,
To write with your hand.
You know you'll leave footprints
In the sand.

When you don't know
Which way to turn,
Put your hands together
You'll surely learn.

Ask your questions
To your soul within,
The truth within answers
Will start to begin.

Escape

When tests may come
Into your life.
Distracting you, I's as if you
Are holding a knife.

When life seems to hold you
Inside a hole,
Forcing you to dig
As if you're a mole.

When you feel as if
There's no way out.
Here's always a ladder
With a saviour to shout.

When you feel as if
You cannot climb,
Just clench your fist,
Then release to be sublime.

You will find the strength,
To climb out of the pits,
Through every single strain,
You'll have help from the spirits.

Directions (Part II)

When love is far,
When the truth will hurt,
When you have battle-scars
Under your shirt.

When you know hard times
Are not far away,
Look to the sky
And embrace the new day.

When you feel empty,
When you feel ill,
Turn the heat up
To get your fill.

When pain inside
Makes you want to hide.
Hold strong to truth
When you see a painful slide.

When anger within
Starts to begin.
Look for truth
And start to swim.

Hard and Tough

Sometimes it's hard
When you feel pain,
Sometimes it's tough
Looking to the rain.

Sometimes it's hard
When emotions clash
Sometimes it's tough
To cope with a rash.

Sometimes I's hard
When there's voices inside.
From Diane and David,
I cannot hide.

Sometimes it's tough
When things go wrong.
Sometimes it's tough
To even listen to a song.

Sometimes it's hard
Being enslaved.
But when you look for truth,
You'll truly be saved.

Directions (Part III)

When you look for help
To fix yourself.
When there's voices around
And even an elf.

When directions direct you
To all the wrong places,
When you seem to see
All the wrong faces,

When you cannot help
The way that you feel,
Knowing full well
That you don't have to steal.

You can hold on strong
To where you belong,
By doing so, you separate.
The rights from wrong.

When you try to impress,
By showing your very best.
When you hold tight to your vest,
You will pass the test.

World Surroundings

Looking Outside,
What do I find?
Inspirational beauty,
Memories of somebody kind.

What do I see
As I look all around?
Safe memories,
Negativity becomes shattered to the ground.

What do I see
When I'm expecting pain?
Goodness and blessings,
Growing the seed into grain.

The sight of beauty
With nature around.
Trees and flowers,
Birds making a sound.

With the light around
With the happiness on earth,
We can all hold a piece of peace
With every single rebirth.

Enemy

What have we done?
We entered a place
Where nobody can even
See our faces, in space.

We know our place,
We know where we stand,
We know who is there
To hold our hand.

We know our family,
Our findings and our kind,
We know the goodness,
If we seek, we will find.

We know the true paths,
We know what's in our way.
We know what holds us.
Every single day.

We have our powers,
We have our field.
With righteous teamwork,
The enemy will yield.

Time (Part XII)

One day, one time,
An opportunity occurred.
To give people a message,
What was noticed, my sound obscured.

A time when a crossroad appears,
A time dark in the midst,
A time when creation
Was down on our list.

A time when DeJaVu
Would be all around,
Almost enough to hold us
To the ground.

A time where time
Is freely restrained,
A time where time
Gets left behind.

A time where time
Can surely break,
A time when people
Would make a mistake.

A time when life
Could be compared
To a time in another life
I had to be prepared.

Christmas

Christmas is here,
The windows have lights,
There's a nativity on the shelf
Holding baby Jesus, that's right.

There's wrapping paper around the presents,
They are placed under a tree.
There's then a star placed on top
For all the children to see.

There's holly in the halls,
There are bells on the walls,
There's mistletoe on the ceiling,
There are plenty of family phone calls.

There are tears to share,
There's love everywhere,
There's a robin in the air,
There's a partridge eating a pear.

There's gravy in a pan,
The oven holds a turkey leg,
There's a trifle in the fridge,
The wall holds a cross on a peg.

There are mince pies for the masses,
Pigs in blankets are cooked so well,
There's mass excitement all around,
The room is filled with a beautiful smell.

With hot chestnuts to be eaten,
With wine in each glass,
We keep inside the true meaning
Of why we celebrate Christmas.

There are chocolates on the table,
The people are being so kind,
Remember the truth whilst celebrating,
Keep the Stable in your mind.

The people start to feast,
They wish for Christmas snow.
Cookies are passed around the table,
The sharing displays a glow.

St. Nicholas is in our thoughts,
An old battery is thrown in the well.
Merry Christmas Everybody,
And don't forget, Emmanuel.

Running Through Time

Back in a time
When we knew what was true
Before paths got scattered
And we knew not what to do.

We were told that it would be hard,
That nobody would believe a spinning ball,
But deep down there was faith
That we would all stand tall.

"it's happening already",
Were the words that were said
While the screams all around
Entered my head.

Additives within the system
Manipulated the mind,
Making us different,
Feeling left behind.

"All we can do is pray and wait"
We can hope for escape,
We can pray for our hero's
To help us fly with no cape.

Whilst given a drink before travel a
s a safety precaution.
With the book of life in my hand
Emotions collide, we're taken to exhaustion.

Sister spelled safety one night
To do what is right
In order to help the light
Win the good fight.

For that I must thank her,
I must send her my praise,
I do what's important
In order to pass through each phase.

With a bite of an apple for breakfast
Which was a childhood memory mistake.
I knew not of my actions
Whilst hunger forced me to take.

No food was essential
For the time travel loop,
In order to jump across
As a soldier type of troop.

I was shouted at for breaking rules
In order to inform me of my flaw,
I just hope that what an older me had saw
Explains what a child me couldn't core.

When the changeover occurred,
And the crown was affixed,
The shattered damage exploding
Caused my emotions to be mixed.

However, due to an appreciated gift,
Which gave me protection,
Responders within my nerve endings
Returned a telepathic affection connection.

Through a Portal (Part II)

To fly out of a portal,
And into a life
With microwaves and toasters,
All the while without a wife.

To seek but to not find,
What was left behind,
I must have been so blind.
I knew I had to be kind.

I did my best,
Looked to the west,
I wore my vest
Holding my heart in my chest.

I heard all the cars.
I grabbed my god heart tool.
I looked to the stars,
People stayed whole.

I knew I had to walk
In a specific direction.
In a positive manner
Whilst showing affection.

I stumbled upon glitches of reality.
I stumbled upon myself.
I looked towards the stars,
I looked for help.

The world I knew was different,
The animals around were close.
I showed love to the souls
Around me, of course.

I erased past demons,
With a gun full of holy water to wash,
Every demonic activity
So, it would soon be squashed.

Childhood (Part II)

During a dream in my late twenties,
I saw a place back in time
When I first started to research.
This is when I started to write a rhyme.

It was a time in my childhood,
I dreamed as I looked for a bag which I own.
I know I shouldn't be there,
But in the present, I have grown.

I learn that my sister
Is waiting in a car outside.
I remain unseen,
I know I must hide.

I walk out of the house,
A connection with nature, I make.
As I open my eyes in my twenties
With memories of these timelines is when I awake.

Dream World (Part II)

As I slept on my sofa,
I had a dream in my head,
I agreed to follow the noise
As I argued with what was said.

I agreed to walk through my hallway,
I opened my front door.
But my stairwell had an extra corridor,
Flipped ninety degrees, I peak to seek more.

Weirdly, I see a known face,
As he walks down the stairs in front, that was there.
I saw that his eyes were so wide,
I turn back into my home, try not to store.

As I headed back through my hallway, And back through the hallway,
And into the kitchen, to my surprise,
I see some pints of beer
Before my eyes.

The beers were dark,
On top was froth,
Suddenly, in ran a shadowed female.
She was as dark as a Goth.

She grabbed a pint so quickly,
Then she ran off, she was so fast.
With a dark aura,
She flew away with a blast.

The last thing I heard was a voice asking
"did he see my face"?
Unfortunately, that jigsaw piece
Had been misplaced.

I awake, and weirdly
The first words that I say
Is "drink", then I hear the words "true love"
But it is the start of a new day.

Through a Struggle

There were a few people
Who showed me a family feel,
I felt brotherly love
And we all knew that it was real.

We went through struggle,
Separately side by side,
We stood strong proudly,
We knew not to hide.

Through financial stress,
We stayed strong,
We proved to the others
That they were all wrong.

We knew to believe,
We knew to stand tall,
We knew that we had to look passed
Each other, overall.

We stand together,
We do what we must,
We unify our forces,
Because it's only just that in God we must trust.

Travelling Between Worlds

During a lifetime
In a world that wasn't this,
I travelled between mirrors
To be able to complete the truth with bliss.

I travelled on a boat,
There was about a dozen onboard,
A wooden rowboat
Inside this memory stored.

There were trees all around, with eyes in the darkness
As we paddled through the stream,
This memory is almost like
It was a mission inside an impossible dream.

As I was sleepy,
Onboard, I lay my head.
Whilst absorbing the lives around me
And listening to what is said.

I was protected as I slept,
There were beings to watch over me,
I knew that there was a mission
In order to be free.

I asked, "will I succeed?"
As the elephant onboard looked inside my mind.
When I eventually woke up, the elephant was crying.
I had no idea what she would find.

I went to comfort,
I want to be true,
Because at the time,
I knew not what to do.

I travelled the world,
I forced my path,
But after memories erased,
I became confused about the aftermath,

Even though I try
To accomplish my deeds,
I do my best to support
Other people's needs.

That may become a weakness,
But see seep inside my heart,
That my weakness is a strength
And because of this, the rollercoaster must start

Trouble in Paradise

To be thrown away,
To be left alone,
Forced to reap the facts
That have been sown.

To be ignored,
To be slaughtered quickly,
Slashed across the face,
The first facts that poured blood thickly.

To learn alone,
To grow in isolation,
Whilst communicating digitally
And on air with the nations.

Even thought I stay alone,
At a home that I built.
Forced to feel
The aftermath of corrupted guilt.

Knowing that a mission,
Would take me too far,
I just wish that there was a soul
Accompanying me at home with a par.

Someone to stay
And not allow me to fall,
Because that's not the route
That I want at all.

Crown

To walk through a path
Where things fell in line,
To synchronise with life
Can sometimes be sublime,

To feel the same
As what I hear,
It can sometimes trigger hopes,
It can sometimes trigger fears.

To hear quantum times music
In time with the cars,
Whilst sitting in an office
Which is also a coffee shop and a whiskey bar.

Holding my laser pen,
Choosing my platform,
I decipher the correct path
In order to reform.

To be aware of the consciousness
With music in time,
Knowing that it links
With past lives with their rhymes.

To be linked with consciousness,
Which spreads worldwide
Whilst being myself,
Alone, I don't want to hide.

When times freeze,
Or even slow down,
You know the truth,
You wear the crown.

Somewhere Else

During a time
When I was wed
After the vows
And after all that was said.

We both went away,
We enjoyed our whole time.
We both had a mountain
That we had to climb.

We went to a casino
We both placed our bets,
We both lived in a time
Even though we both had regrets.

We reached a room
Where we would seal the deal,
But due to different reasons
We had such a strange feel.

Out of the tights,
There came a knife,
Betrayal was felt,
I was almost stabbed by my wife.

With my defence,
I stopped the stab.
I removed the hazard
And it felt so fab,

Off she then wandered,
She had secrets to keep
She betrayed my trust
This is what made me weep.

We both got home,
I was prepared.
But because of the influence of fear
She made me so scared.

Arguments begun,
We lost our home,
I found my house,
It became the new norm.

She bossed her divorce,
And tried to remove my land.
But thanks to my family,
I had a well-deserved helping hand.

Through this betrayal,
It all came to an end,
I was left to deal with my heartache
Without a single friend.

I then came to learn,
That my heart had true painful pain.
It was due to the death of my loved one
Which is what drove me insane.

I was hated by her family,
I was exiled due to my love.
But I wanted to make it right
As I prayed to above.

I released her from my heart
Through this pain, her halves were reunited.
I knew that the same would happen to me
As my death would be one day ignited.

Sever

When things get hard,
When people don't comply,
When diseases start to spread
And people wonder why.

When mess begins to form,
When disgrace is all around
It's time to take it back
And throw it to the ground.

When wrongs become right,
Even when it feels so wrong.
We gather all that we have
And throw it in a song.

When people don't seem to care,
When people hide their face,
When people spoil the earth
It then becomes a disgrace.

When negativity falls,
When all is unclear,
We start to work together
To sever what we fear.

Isolation & Loneliness

Sometimes when people
Are left all alone
With nobody to talk to,
Whilst watching the phone.

It can be tough to gather
Emotions inside
With no sort of help,
It makes you want to hide.

The feeling of loneliness
Can depress a person's soul.
Restricting themselves
From becoming whole.

Isolation can hurt,
It can cause heartache.
It can change your emotions,
It can keep you awake.

When loneliness will settle,
You just want to run.
To find a little less isolation.
As a remedy, a cure, some fun.

Do not be isolated,
It can tear you apart.
Find yourselves, good friends,
Find a brand-new start.

External Factors

When your actions contradict
The emotions you feel.
Making you wonder
What is real.

Feeling victimised by surroundings,
Being compromised from within.
It restricts your ability
To restart and begin.

External factors
Can pull people to the ground,
It can influence your actions,
It can create a butterfly effect around.

Internal manipulation
Can be forced into the mind.
To keep people stuck
In a negative emotion, keeping us blind.

Both women and men
Can be controlled from outside.
But even if we foul,
We can at least say that we tried.

We must work together for the sake of defences
To fight the evil influences.
We must block them out and lock all our fences
Eventually we can release all the past tenses.

Be true to yourself,
Do what you must do.
Think of all as your family,
You can eventually pull through.

Seasons

The summer is here,
The sun shines bright,
It beams through the earth
Until early the next night.

The birds are now singing
The bees on the flowers,
Creating many beauties
For hours upon hours.

The clocks will fall back,
The leaves start to fall.
The nights will grow darker,
Daytime activities will stall.

The sky turns quite cloudy,
The storms will begin,
The doors will get locked
As the nights will begin.

Christmas time is coming,
We celebrate the special time.
We are trimming the ceiling,
Up the tree we start to climb.

The new year will pass,
Resolutions are made.
Memories of the past
Soon starts to fade.

The spring will arrive,
Even if we hurt our spleen.
It will not stop us
From having our spring clean.

Creative Activities

When you're stuck in a rut,
When you're left on your own.
When you're lucky to escape,
When your feelings have grown.

When emotions are suppressed,
You feel it in your chest.
You try to do what is best,
You leave out all the rest.

When you struggle to escape
Or express how you feel,
You try to find a way,
To express the feelings that is real.

You may find a pen,
Some paint or some work,
You try to keep yourself busy,
Even if it drives you bezerk.

You may draw a picture,
You may write a story,
It may be about pain,
Or even about glory.

You may express emotions,
You may express pain,
You may express joy,
It may drive you insane.

You create what you see,
Whatever it may be,
You may draw a beautiful tree,
Do whatever sets you free.

The Reality of the yellow Skin

As I go to the store
And I walk down the aisle.
There are many of these
All stacked in a pile.

Some are green,
Some are brown,
Some are yellow,
All in the same town.

Some can be healthy,
Some can be bad,
Some can be bitty,
But there are good ones and I'm glad.

Some can be big,
Some can be small,
Monkeys like to eat them,
But not from the shopping mall.

They grow on trees,
You can slip on the peel,
You may not believe me
But bananas are real.

Poverty

It can be hard to walk
And see people in poverty,
They know their troubles,
Can contradict people so truly.

To see the lack of ability,
To provide for their friends,
Whilst knowing it's hard.
Hoping that it will come to an end.

No money for travel,
No money for food,
No money for a home,
Living in a troublesome brood.

They look for a change,
They look to advance,
They look to survive
They have a true glance.

They look for some help
From government officials on their stools.
But the rich cannot see
Whilst swimming in their private pool.

The contradictions show
How unfair things are,
While the suffering walk past
A black Mercedes car.

When someone can afford
More than one home
It's clear that it's time
To change the norm.

Social Gathering at a Job Club.

Some people struggle
To put words together,
Some people try
To make themselves better.

Some people want
To update their work,
Some want experience,
Some feel like a jerk.

Some people need help
To use a PC
Some people just want
To update their CV.

Some people's faith
Can become corrupted.
Sometimes temptation
Can cause their path to be interrupted.

Sometimes people
Look for some guidance,
Sometimes people
Just build up a fence.

Sometimes people want
A social gathering,
Sometimes people pass
Because they wing the best of something.

Sometimes people
Need to look up above.
And find truth in God
To find their true love.

The Chair (Part II)

When I get home
With an achy feel,
Trying to understand
What is real.

I look to the corner
With tea in my hand.
I slowly start to pace
As I try to understand.

I ignore propaganda,
I block out all the pain,
I know this destination
Could drive me insane.

As I leap back in time
With my memories in a loop,
As a soldier, I march.
I feel like a troop.

I gather my stationary, my paper,
I comb back my hair.
I then start to write
In my incredible, awesome chair.

C.A.P

Flashing colours,
Advertisements around
All used to keep
The people on the ground.

Mobile phones and internet,
Computers and loans,
Keeping people trapped in groans,
Forcing people to stay in their homes.

Suddenly they are stuck
In a pickle, in a rut.
Not knowing where to go
Suppressing the pains in their gut.

Sometimes when their stuck,
They feel like they're in a trap,
They want to grow wings
To fly away with a flap.

But lucky for them,
There's help, out there.
Decent help from these people,
All showing that they care.

With a management plan
To help them pull through,
Just call C.A.P,
They know what to do.

Thereafter

Taking a break,
Enjoying a drink,
Looking inside,
Having a think

Finding directions,
Finding what's true.
Wondering which path
On the crossroad is true.

Marching on swiftly,
Keeping inside,
Keeping control,
Holding your pride.

Starting a laugh,
Sharing a smile.
Knowing inside
It can take such a long while.

You start at the beginning,
You look towards the end,
You may want to be a millionaire,
You may just want to phone a friend.

Ideas get shared,
Through a subconscious thought.
You look through some items
That you previously bought.

Looking for happiness,
Avoiding disaster.
Knowing you'll be rewarded
With what comes thereafter.

Somewhere Inside.

Pick up a pen,
Hold a notepad,
Holding all feelings
Both happy and sad.

Feeling inside,
Not knowing what will be, really,
Just allowing information
To flow out so freely

Gathering inside my thoughts,
Feeling them connect.
Placing them together like a jigsaw,
Whilst holding self respect.

Spreading positive cheer,
Whilst unaware how come.
Realising that emotions
Inside can become numb.

Allow the mind to flow,
Realise what you feel,
Explain your emotions,
Whilst knowing what's real.

Keeping yourself calm,
Keep in control.
Express your emotions,
It can be one for all.

Where it can come from,
Somewhere inside.
These suppressed emotions
Sometimes like to hide.

Spring

The leaves are yellow
As they start to grow.
The clouds start to clear,
The sun starts to show.

The clocks go forward,
The nights then get short.
The flowers will emerge,
Through the seeds of thought.

The yellow sun is shining,
It causes a yellow glow in the air.
The birds are all singing,
The bread, they all share.

People's hair starts to bleach
As they walk through the town,
Some people are in t-shirts and shorts.
Some people are out in their dressing gown.

Sandals are unpacked,
In preparation for months to come.
Getting ready for the summer,
The spring has now begun.

Three Lives and a Symphony from Hell

There was a time
Before this time
Where I would sit down
Writing a rhyme,
I would listen to music
Without committing a crime,
I'd absorb the abuse,
It felt all sublime.

I'd hear the voices,
I would accept what it true,
Because I knew the ending,
I knew that I'd pull through.
I kept myself strong,
I knew what to do.
I kept on believing,
For "you know who".

That person was living
In a simulated life,
She was taken from her true home
She was my runaway wife.
She protected herself
With a stake-like knife.
But I stayed strong,
You may call it strife.

No matter what happened,
Knowing that there was no tech,
She stayed in the darkness,
She remained a pain in my neck,
Even though she tried to break me,
I knew I couldn't remain a wreck.

Without the machine,
I made my plan,
Knowing that she
Would forget who I am.
She acts like a child,
If I could only get her a pram.
Or if she decided to scratch my door.
I may say "scram".

But due to the hypnotics,
The life ended back then.
I knew I would restart
And have a chance to begin again.
Between the first life and the second,
She refused a lot of men.
She slashed them like a chicken
Because I was a hen.

My second life then started,
Machines were all around
Cables and wires.
They were buried underground.
Satellite dishes,
All emitting sound.
Due to all of this,
You wouldn't believe what we found.

We failed the second life happily,
We were sent to hell,
I was then there to witness
My wife had a second bell.
But it was with a vampire,
She fell.
Unfortunately, in this third life,
She acted like she couldn't tell.

So, this life then started,
Things began all wrong,
I worked so hard
To find my hidden song.
People condemned me,
They said I didn't belong.
Unfortunately for them,
I proved that I was no mong.

This song, I created.
It would last such a long time, you know?
But I came prepared,
With each chapter to be shown.
People didn't believe me,
But these feelings would grow.
As I brought back my symphony from hell.

Disaster~tunity (can I change the time?)

One day, there was a disaster
During the earthly breakdown.
There was a long walk
To return to my hometown.

It took weeks on end
And many miles were crossed.
Throughout the journey,
Many emotions were lost.

We got home,
It was a blackout.
After we fixed the lights
People started to shout.

The table holding a television
Shattered upon a spark,
It made such a loud noise,
I don't know if I heard a dog bark.

Glass shattered everywhere,
My hands covered my face.
But many things survived the incident,
But I still had a sad look in my place.

I told the people to not touch gadgets,
But someone didn't listen to me.
During being traced, the home was under attack,
I hoped that it couldn't be.

After I was alerted by an alarm
That I would then own.
We knew we had to leave,
Before bigger alarms had been shown.

During this time,
Bitcoin had its rise,
And quite easily, I became wealthy,
To my own surprise.

I withdrew my money,
Before the stocks would fall.
But due to this mistake,
They climbed much higher than previously, after all.

An Exploding Earth

After my second life,
I knew I passed the test,
I hoped because
Somebody else knew best.

I sat back and watched
As I pressed the button which was red.
After listening to the information
That was previously fed.

In my madness,
In my hope,
A disaster occurred,
It made me mope.

I was there to witness
Something so bad.
But I was told it was alright,
Even though it drove me mad.

I said "I didn't want them to die"
Which they replied with, don't worry, now's your chance.
I took their word, I looked forward
Without a second glance.

The thing that happened
What made me cry
Was when I saw
The earth's goodbye.

There I was,
Outside the firmament,
I felt so helpless
For the time that I spend.

I said, "I've been tricked",
But I had to see
What would happen if I didn't
Return to set the truth free.

1, 2, Skip a Few, 29, 30

When entering this world,
This simulated reality
We listened to the voices
Created by integrity.

The system handed a blueprint,
Placed before my eyes.
They explained the entire situation,
Yes, I was rather surprised.

I was told "it's very cleverly built"
Whist looking at the firmament diagram which was blue.
I was explained that it would be difficult
But we could pull through.

I was told about the distance
Between a being and what can fly.
From the day I was torn,
I must have needed help from the sky.

Past scenes and memories
Were sure to be erased.
While difficult challenges were in our faces
Would surely be placed.

Eventually the distance
Would become less
And where the person is,
I couldn't hazard to guess.

We knew we must turn back,
We knew what must be done.
But due to her addiction to lust, which wasn't mine.
I couldn't prove one thing.

Due to being labelled
And painted all over by others,
I hope that my traitorous abandonment is understood
When I see my mothers.

Preparing for the Game (Part I)

Here I am
In a dark room,
The lights are dim,
I'm feeling gloom.

I write many lyrics,
I put it on paper,
The lyrics are recorded,
It tapes me and tapes her.

We are very clever with grammar,
We avoid the "disaster".
We place the words in the machine.
Over and over, we "pass" much faster.

We create music
In preparation for life.
We avoid more disasters,
We don't need a knife.

We pay with coins
Used from a treasure chest.
We do things right
Because we know what's best.

We prepare to enter this world
By any means necessary.
We make our plans
To escape what's planetary.

The room is lit
By candle light,
Free energy is then created
With all our might.

We use the looking glass
To watch over an event,
Knowing our mission
Involves both people to repent.

I used clocks and other items
To time my entire world
Until other means were available
Discovered by somebody else, how obscured.

When my company arrived,
It became easy to see
How important this mission
Is to both her and, yes… me.

Dream Girl

After I left
This place on earth,
Before I had a chance
To have my re-birth.

A dream girl that I know,
I saw her once again.
She tried to ask me
As I stood on this train.

I saw her face,
She wondered if I felt love,
Or if it was a lustful feeling.
So, I looked above.

When I realised that
Those feelings weren't true.
It was time for a change,
Something else to do.

When I was reborn,
Then thirty years later.
It was during a time
When I became a skater.

I dreamed of this girl,
During a strange night.
She brought back some memories
As my eyes has a delightful fright.

Ghosts (Part V)

One night, at my home
I was feeling down.
I walked to seek a way
To eliminate my frown.

I trekked through my hallway.
And by my living room door.
I saw bubbles floating
About a metre above the floor.

The blue one was prominent,
It was so bright,
I couldn't avoid it
With all my might.

I reached my doubtless
Incredible, amazing chair.
As I looked out my window
And saw a ghost standing there.

I also spotted a green orb
Flying in my bedroom, it's true.
It was so much brighter
Than the one that was blue.

My cat and I
Watched this green ball,
Then my cat, Ninja chased it
Into the crucifix on my wall.

After years of haunting
And years of fear,
I decided to record them
To make it all clear.

I set up four cameras
And conference called them all,
A ghost walked through one of them,
It broke one camera and ended the call.

Lucky for me,
I captured the figure of a ghost.
It was an unusual guest,
I was an unusual host.

I captured a red figure
Stood by my door,
But I missed the orbs on this night,
They weren't floating above the floor.

But there were no worries
As I looked to my town.
When I captured a ghost gun
As well as a ghost crown.

Free Falling (Part II)

So, I reached the skies,
I saw three tubes suspended high up there.
My eyes were filled with fright,
I couldn't help but stare.

Inside one pod
Was my son and his mother,
I saw my first wife in one
And my second wife in anther.

I was told to make a choice,
It was a difficult choice to make.
Because I loved them all.
I gave my life, it wasn't fake.

I turned to my right,
I bolted off the cloud,
I headed towards the earth,
This I say aloud.

I was once so high,
High above it all.
This is the story
About a hazardous free-fall.

Preparing for the Game (Part II)

Before I entered
This simulation,
A deal was made
Which included all the nation.

If I could be freed,
So could the rest.
I knew that I'd try
To do what is best.

All the family
Is held inside.
But due to the severity
I could not hide.

I was told
That all I had to do
Was survive myself.
And the others would too.

The mission at hand
Is to free all who's trapped.
This is the information
That has now been lapped.

So, the mission is clear
What I need to be.
Is true to myself
And we can all be free.

Judgment

During the judgment,
Surrounded by voices,
Images and faces,
So many noises.

The courtroom is large,
The biggest of all.
I must be righteous
To avoid the free fall.

I see every moment,
Every memory.
I see what I must do
In order to be free.

Every single pixel,
No longer tunnel vision.
Every hidden thing,
Inside my mission.

Every regret, every moment,
Comes back in my mind.
Reminding me of all
The things that are unkind.

All the moments that hurt
Revealed once more.
I live it over again
To prepare me for the next door.

After the bad stuff,
Here comes Grace
To remind me of the good stuff
It's then slapped across my face.

I see the good,
I know that I'm nice,
Anybody who disputed my actions
Needs to think twice.

I do good things,
If that's a crime, then I'm guilty.
But if I get locked away for that,
Please keep me warm with a quilt, see?

Hackers in my Mind

As I'm thinking,
As I write,
Voices interrupt me.
Yeah, that's right.

I think to myself
Then interruptions "pop in"
Intruding my mind,
Stopping me from being able to begin.

Persecuting my thoughts,
Intruding in my brain,
Doing what they please,
Driving me insane.

They feel like they have the right
To instigate negative responses.
But if they think they can control me,
Then they are just a bunch on nonces.

The truth that I say
Is that this harassment is real,
And I pray that grace can find
The good that they may feel.

Claiming my repellents
Are my fault, alone.
When the intoxicating chemical they consume is flaunted.
Their true evil has grown, and now it's shown.

I pray for their health,
Their repentance alike.
Otherwise, hypocrites they are
And they deserve to be on their bike.

Bubbles (Part II)

There was a time
Before what is known,
Where I lived in a bubble
It can sometimes be shown.

I watched my own life
From outside my window,
Knowing the truth
As it starts to show.

I hear the noise
Of drilling all around.
Jackhammers and workers
All working on the ground.

Inside these bubbles,
I stay with my friends.
We play word games
Our fun seems to never end.

Then the male voice
Who usually seems kind
Says something different,
A different meaning is what I'd find.

Due to this issue,
I didn't feel safe to stay there,
I jumped out of the bubble
To prepare to show that I care.

The bubble life ended,
I went elsewhere in time
I swam to the blue
And this is the follow-up rhyme.

Playtime (Part II)

I was told that I had a chance
To participate in a play,
I was told this
On one dark like day.

In order to succeed,
I would have to survive
In a virtual racing game
Racing with others as I drive.

As people would fail,
They would die.
But I had some advice
To help me get by.

During this radical race,
I saw the look on the face
Of the others as they lost their place
They got blasted and zapped. To end them, just in case.

I was advised to stay
On the blue line,
If I did that,
I was told I'd e fine.

I was told about the corners
And where I shouldn't go.
But the race was different,
It didn't keep me off the floor.

When I succeeded,
I told my family.
But they were upset,
I sadly now see.

They rightfully freaked out,
My sisters helped me as I laid down.
As they put a spell in my heart,
I didn't want to frown.

They told me that the spell
Would protect my soul,
I believed them
They assured me that I'd feel whole.

I was told on that night
Not to eat a thing.
I knew to be a strong child
And to stay courageous within.

Unfortunately, hunger
Got the best of me,
I went to the kitchen
To see what I could see.

My mother noticed
That I had a bite,
I tried to flush it out
With all my might.

As I went into the room,
I drank from the grail.
Not knowing what
The truth would unveil.

I got close to death,
Then a voice within
Reminded me of what is good.
And I knew not to give in.

I then heard a voice
During the interchange.
Saying "I guess there was good in him after all"
This time was strange.

The morale of that last verse
Proves their intentions were to slay.
But unfortunately for them,
They wait while I stay.

Everything in Between

Every day
Is the worst day ever.
Whilst simultaneously the best,
Isn't that clever?

It's a nice feeling,
It also feels so wrong.
So, I thought I'd put it
Into a different song.

It makes me feel bad
And it makes me feel good.
Exactly as it shouldn't,
Exactly as it should.

Even though I feel worse,
It makes me feel better.
So, I thought I'd write it
On a letter.

Thinking about it,
It makes me feel down.
But it raises me up
Like a king without a crown.

Whilst dealing with it all,
I get stuck in the middle.
So why not play along
With your very own fiddle?

When I First Met Cheyenne

During a time
When I was a king,
I had my Queen,
She wore my ring.

But due to her
Lack of faithfulness and love
She betrayed me,
She cheated on the above.

This forced me
Into depression
So, I walked out
To learn a lesson.

On my journey,
I then met the "Cheyenne Girl"
That's when my story.
Had begun a new whirl.

We made love,
It seemed so true,
But when I returned to my kingdom,
I knew not what to do.

Dream World (Part III)

In a dream
With my son and my mother,
I saw a sign for Disney
And then I saw another.

My son wanted to enter
Into a swimming pool.
But the pool had no water
So, I said the smaller one was cool.

I told my mum
That Disney was 140 pounds,
Then she said "with a voucher,
It's 40 pounds", this brought a different sound.

I looked on cereal boxes
And I found vouchers for this deal.
Who would have thought
That I'd find it on a meal?

Then I teleported,
In a storm, I rocked on a ship,
A whirlpool caused by a dragon
Caused my thick lip.

My father and I
Would seek to find our boat,
There may have been words
Which were stuck in our throat.

I asked the dream girl
Who was stood by a staircase cage,
If I could sit inside,
But she said "no", so I got out without rage.

I explain to the dream girl
That our ship had been capsized,
Then I asked, "where could I find it?"
Before she replied.

"I do not know,
But I'd like to go south".
These were the words
That came out of her mouth.

She had distinctive facial features
On her left cheek.
It was memorable to me,
This is the words that I speak.

I walk up tower street,
She enters a house.
I say, "she was a nice lady".
Before she becomes as silent as a mouse.

I got back to my father
Who is sat in my chair,
"I wish I had a compass"
Are the words that he's shares.

It's a good job that I always have mine"
Are the words I reply,
I pull it out,
The mission, I try.

I hold it vertical,
Infra-red it will shine.
Then I turn it horizontal,
It's bright green now, this is mine.

I see my father,
Looking through maps of many,
I don't know where to start,
I didn't hold a penny.

He rolls a spliff made of solid,
Even though in this reality, we don't touch it.
Then he rolls it b y himself
And hands me a little bit.

"if gran knew about this,
She would shout at me", he said as we moved along
So, I replied "I think that she'd be happy
That we are getting along."

Then I awake,
I didn't smoke in my dream, I lost the clip
But one thing that remained in reality
Was that I still had a fat lip.

Into Different Worlds

When I walked
Inside the cave,
I saw my partner
In a deathly grave.

I jacked myself back in
Because she was stuck,
If I unplugged her,
She'd be out of luck.

I had to enter
Because she had already been spliced.
Into a different world,
In again, this makes twice.

The first time was just a teaser,
But the story had begun
Her lust had been implanted
She went back for a little more fun.

I knew she had entered
Because of this lust,
But a rescue mission was forced
Because it was just.

I can't take her free will,
I can do what just feels right.
So, I tried my very best
With all my might.

She chose the false reality
Over the kingdom of our own,
It gets written down,
To sever what is sown.

She made her wish
To be all alone,
While I granted it in sadness
I remained on my own.

In order not to follow
The same path to hell,
The truth that I know,
I must tell.

But due to past mistakes
When I went down,
I met some vampires
Who invaded my town.

They wish to lead me back to hell
Again, and again
Through infra red Nazi manipulation
Used to drive me insane.

But because of these memories
I will not give in,
I hold Gods faith
Inside me, deep within.

Because of this,
My objective became clear,
Into this world
To eliminate what I fear.

They claim that their life
Is godly and true,
The only truth is that their soul is missing,
Their jealousy forces them to renew.

Without the ability to see the other side,
They only see what is dark,
They have no way to enter
Into Gods kingdom park.

Dream World (Part IV)

I was there in a dream,
On a chair where I was sat,
I felt quite drunk,
I go down the stairs to let in my cat.

I then learn
That she's already inside,
We return upstairs together
Without a need to hide.

As I lay on my bed
Still dreaming in my mind,
The voices fade in and out,
Is what I will truly find.

I go to the living
Because I hear people on a date,
I then go to the planetarium
Because it's in my fate.

I lay down
With my head on the floor,
My feet are elevated,
My head is by the door.

I keep my distance
To give the people I hear some space
But the voices are growing,
Perceive the look upon my face.

They call me "Iagor"
Because of the different insides that I possess,
"That is not my name"
Are the words that I confess.

Then somehow the scenery
Has changed within,
I teleport to another property,
The strangeness will begin.

I go to the rooftop,
I walk through a metal gate,
The image I saw
Was unimaginably great.

There was a lady, her hair was red.
She wanted to take control.
But I did not accept her hunger
Because I sensed her call for a fall.

Then before I knew it,
There's a knock on my door.
I pass a dark-haired man
Who is stood on my floor.

I open the door
Where I saw my friend,
In hope that this
Nightmare would soon end.

He asks me who
The lady is upstairs,
I tell him not to worry,
Because my heart cares.

I ask him if he has eaten,
Because eaten, I have not.
I lead him back outside
To return to what I've got.

I teleport once again,
I'm now in a Wordsworth gardens house
I lead myself downstairs,
The place is as quiet as a mouse.

As I reach downstairs
To get myself a treat,
A sandwich by the freezer
I fill it full of meat.

I head to the hallway,
The man is stood there,
I direct him away for protection,
I tell him to go upstairs.

I try to turn on the lights witch a few times,
But it doesn't come on.
So, I return to the kitchen
To discover that my food has gone.

I quickly get more food
But then, I turn around
To see the darkened family.
The red-haired lady is holding my sons' hand, this is what I found.

I drop to my knees and call his name
And my son then walks to me.
He gives me a hug,
But then, I did see.

Two holes in his neck,
Vampire bites on the right,
I give him a hug
In hope that all will be alright.

The two head towards the door to leave,
I tell them to "Take Care"
Because that is the language
That I believe is "Fair".

"Thank you, Mr and Mrs Daniels."
Is what my son would then say,
Then I ask them "did you tell him your names?"
And they say "No", but he knew through some way.

As they leave the building,
Whilst still holding my son,
I see his eyes become swollen,
This sadness has begun.

His neck turns black,
Like some kind of parasite.
It was enough to wake me up
From this evil awful fright.

Then as I awake,
The voices will return.
Now, you know who I are.
I.R meaning infra red is what I learn.

Journey Through Time

After I reached
Another location,
My arms were severed to feed
Two people in a different nation.

"the arms of the fallen
Is the best on the menu".
That is the words that was spoken
To the people in this venue.

The mother and a child consumed
But they were unaware.
"Look for my tattoos." I announced.
That's when they showed true care.

They were put off their food
So, they offered "Cat" instead.
But deception was this mission,
The truth filled their stomach with dread.

The meal wasn't feline,
It was indeed a child.
But the DNA was passed through,
This may have drove them wild.

In order to cure their hunger,
They were offered a deceptive gift
But without their stomach
They had no love to lift.

Now somewhere, I am armless.
The devil asks me to sign,
I explain that I cannot
And he proclaims that it will be fine.

Down through the madness,
Someone donated an arm.
For righteous reasons,
I tell them to keep calm.

Now she has one arm,
But someone donates their own.
Our bodies are mutilated,
But our ideas have grown.

I ask "is it possible for them
To have a robotic arm instead?"
And to our amazement,
This wish was granted.

Back to the place
Where a signature is needed,
Even though I refused to sign,
The arm was controlled on my behalf, after I pleaded.

Now, I'm on a journey,
I'm in purgatory,
In search for my loved ones
To be able to survive in victory.

Another arm gets donated,
Once again, I have another hand.
Down below, they ask for another robot arm,
But apparently, they are in demand.

As I walk through the desert,
I finally reach a portal-like gate,
As I stroll into hell
I see another righteous mission in my fate.

Deception and rat burgers,
Sales and lights of red.
I know to avoid temptation,
The mission continues instead.

Walking Through Hell

When I walked through the gate
Into hell I did reach.
With a righteous mission
In my heart, I would preach.

I was suspended by people
Who wanted me dead.
They gathered around me,
They had their sights on my head.

When a cloaked person
Approached the crown
And proclaimed that I was already owned,
She said it out loud.

She forced away the crown,
I was owned by her.
The agreement was made
As I started to stare.

I'm in a strange twist of fate,
Trust is what I felt.
I followed her with pride,
I remembered my belt.

I take her hand
We walk together
Into a location
That seemed to last forever.

She handed me a cloak
Because our destination was unsafe for man.
We headed off together
Because she had a plan.

In another twist,
I needed a disguise.
In a location of bloodthirsty women,
New clothes were in front of my eyes.

I was made to wear new clothing,
Like a lady, I would look.
In order to survive,
There was a new mission in this book.

We reached the location
That was safe at the time.
But due to a mistake,
We had to leave, a new quest I was forced to climb.

Remember the Mission (Part III)

As I'm stood in the clouds,
I'm filled with reasons to hate.
The person I love
In a strange twist of fate.

Through deception and manipulation,
I'm forced to realise.
That she broke me in pieces
Without a surprise.

Because of the feeling
That was forced upon me,
I'm convinced to let her go
In order to be free.

Not to sever her is the mission,
Yet, I must escape her hold.
But the realisation kicked in
A story of sorrow is now told.

I never intended
For death to take over,
So, I approached her
Faster than a land rover.

I brought her back to life
With the kiss of true love,
Her eyes then opened
As I cried, whilst kneeling above.

After the commotion,
The perpetrator was unmasked, at last.
As his head is removed
As he's sent to the past.

Now due to this past life,
The memory has been planted.
I pray to above
That the wish of salvation will be granted.

With the memory to stop
It all before it's placed.
The truth of knowledge
Is placed upon y face.

The one who was killed
For breaking my heart
Is the one I must save
At the very start.

In the Skies

When I approached Mary
I told her that I couldn't stay,
Because I had another mission
Heading towards me in my play.

When I passed her the news,
She shed tears, so sad.
I felt so sorry,
It drove me so mad.

Due to the pain
That I could see,
Knowing I couldn't bare
What would be.

I left the scene
For her to find her way,
As I continued my mission
That was placed in my play.

Now, knowing what happened,
If she was offered at the end.
I surely would take her
To eternally be my friend.

Inside the Contact Lenses

When there's no eye contact,
I cannot trust
Because I know not the emotions,
I know there may be lust.

I keep my distance
Because I cannot see.
The windows of the soul
That could set us free.

Without eye contact,
I cannot tell if you are lying.
Without eye contact,
I know not if you're laughing or crying.

Even if you do,
Look deep inside my soul,
Do not spread venom
Or you won't be whole.

Abusive behaviour and negativity
I will not accept in my heart.
It's the kind of thing
That will force us apart.

If you fill me
With abuse
Then all you are doing
Is tightening your noose.

If you condemn me
As you stare.
I'll look back
With a comical glance.

If you betray me
Or persecute,
Rest assured, you'll need
A hefty parachute.

With lack of faith
Shot into my flesh,
You will see
Beyond this mesh.

Excuses and alibi's
Will get you nowhere.
All it will get you
Is an empty stare.

Fraudsters and hypocrites
Trying to preach.
As they stare at me
Again, I'll say no. that's what I teach.

The Replacement

When I leave the apartment
And into the house,
In preparation to repent,
A female moves into number eleven wearing a blue blouse.

Her name begins with "M",
She dreamed of this place
A long time ago,
Like DeJaVu on her place.

As I'm living in my bubble
Before this happened to start.
I saw this lady
Before we drifted apart.

A true saint within,
The story will remain alive.
Redemption is upon us,
The slackers cannot skive.

The Arrival

When the newbies
Would finally arrive,
I felt the love of a family,
It made me feel alive.

I told my parents
Of the light I could feel,
Because I knew deep down
That something was real.

Unfortunately for me,
Mixed messages were passed.
Instigating violence
Between the families, at last.

The sister hated me
With no reason behind her blind eyes,
She called the police
In hope of my goodbyes.

Unfortunately for her,
And her lack of information.
She couldn't lock me away
With the criminals of the nation.

Even though I was kind
And provided the family with an unwanted key,
It still wasn't enough
For them to be kind to me.

With anger and rage,
I was forced into a cage.
So, I'm setting the stage
As I turn the page.

They tried to capitalise
On my silly mistake
Because I would smoke,
They pulled out their stake.

They complained of noise
As they yelled, they stomped on my head.
Instigating depression
And forcing my dread.

They were the ones
Who consumed chemicals from a can, inside.
The foul-mouthed hypocrites
Have no place to hide.

Innocent

In a random timeline
Where revenge is upon me,
Reinforcements are called
For the whole world to see.

The police arrive,
I get taken away,
The smile on their faces
Makes their day.

At the time of enlightenment,
I show what I collected.
And due to the truth,
I'm differently respected.

I go home,
They are now free.
With nowhere to go,
I can finally be me.

The middle of the story,
Is that you must repent.
And not suck the blood
Of the innocent.

Remember the Mission (Part IV)

In a life where I was born through caesarean,
My life was unique,
I could communicate with "The Mother"
Through telepathic mystique.

Through a deception at a fairground,
A devilish game,
As a child, I was convinced
To enter this game.

During simulation number one,
Machines weren't to be fund.
There was no music,
N deception to be found.

Figs would be collected,
Time with nature was spent.
With my loved one I lived,
There was no need to repent.

We moved to a house,
She fell for lust,
This caused my bitterness,
Alright, the severing, we don't trust.

After escaping
Through love and what's true,
Our souls were saved
So, we'd know what to do.

But because of the things that had happened,
My soul was missing from me,
So, a chance to redeem
Was a plan to set us free.

When we returned
To life number two,
Things was different,
The machines were all new.

After that life,
Surely, we'd fail
Because without a soul
To guide us on our trail.

The severing occurred,
Down to hell we went
Because of the things
We couldn't repent.

This time, down there
My mission was in my stare,
I was to reclaim my original soul
To make things fair.

I used my original soul
As collateral to return
And now that I'm back
There are new things to learn.

On earth I would stand,
My one true self I would feel.
In order to escape
Back to a place that is real.

Torture in Hell

I was in hell,
I was forced to feel pain.
A devil and a female
Trying to drive me insane.

Inflicting damage
Hurting my inside,
Knowing that I
Had no place to hide.

Torture and suffering
Was inflicted upon me
Forcing tears
For all to see.

After time of endurance
And feeling what was happening,
I knew I could handle it
With a whole new beginning.

Whilst awaiting the torture,
One day did arrive.
I was no longer scared,
I didn't want to drive.

Instead, I enjoyed,
As I asked for more,
I loved every moment
Deep inside my core.

Because of the love
For myself I would feel.
I was taken away
To enjoy earth's meal.

A Bad Day

My alarm clock bleeps,
I fall out of bed.
Unfortunately for me,
I have a bruise on my head.

I stumble to the clock
I stub my toe.
Then trip over my clothes,
On the way to the door.

I head to the toilet
And pee on my feet.
Then I get aftershave in my eyes
As I prepare to greet.

I put on my clothes
And fall out the door.
I stumble down the stairs
And fall to the floor.

I walk outside,
I get sunburned.
Because my sun cream is at home,
I guess I have learned.

I trip over a cat
And I scratch my face.
Now I'm in
A bloody disgrace.

I get a plaster,
But due to allergy
I came out in a rash
For everyone to see.

I hope to heal,
I look to the sky,
But as luck would have it,
A bird poops in my eye.

I wipe it clean,
But there's oil on the rag.
Now my eye is black
So, from my cigarette, I take a drag.

But the filter gets
Stuck in my lips,
I accidently swallow it,
Now it must pass through my hips.

Unfortunately for me,
I'm now running late.
So, I move along faster
Because I have a date.

I arrive early
But she doesn't show.
Where she is,
I do not know.

I look north,
I look east,
I then realise
That my t-shirt is creased.

Due to complications,
I go home to be free.
But I realise that I'm locked out
Because I lost my key.

A Werewolf and a Vampire Trapped in a Safety Box

On one side there's a werewolf,
On the other there's a vampire.
Both contained for safety,
Whilst protected by a force who is higher.

In the place of safety
They must remain
In order to stop the conflict
We will remain.

Through hope and fear,
Through strife and bravery,
We control ourselves,
We try to escape slavery.

When the time does come
To release what's inside,
The entire cavalry must be present,
Protection to all, abide.

Through what's on our home,
We work together for protection,
We all do what we can
In order to reduce the need for correction.

Deception

The way things are shown
Through subliminal messages on TV
By media outlets
Who advertise towards reality.

It can be difficult
To percept the concept of prices
And the ability of the forces
Who like to use alternate dices.

Minds get distracted
It throws confusion to the masses.
Which try to gather money
By using all their passes.

By draining it all
Into a specific source.
Risks leaving our trust
In an unknowing force.

Most companies,
Owned by few,
Step by step,
We find what's true.

Praying Aloud

When we settle down
And we finally find peace
We can learn,
We can find our release.

We harmonise with earth,
Our heartbeat becomes one.
We lay in love, like an angel from above.
We know our journey has begun.

We restart ourselves,
We project our life.
We spread our cheer,
With all our might.

We look to the right
After look into our left side.
We march ahead
With no need to hide.

With courage we stand,
We're humble and proud.
Holding rage in control
Whilst praying aloud.

A Dark Night

It was a cold wind
On a mysterious night
A stormy feeling
Brought such a sight.

The people are crowded,
The air is dark,
Red lights and barriers,
There's nowhere to park.

The crowds are in fear,
They hope to pass the gate.
While those in the middle
Hoping that it's not too late.

Some are infected
In different ways to others.
People all around
Fathers and mothers.

The guards are controlling,
There are orders from the military personnel.
They keep their division between the people
Who don't seem to dispel.

Black armour and helmets
Both batons and spray.
We are fighting for unity
To find the way.

A Royal Time

There was a king and a queen
They both had dark hair.
They'd look after the people
With the riches they share

One unfortunate day
The wife went astray,
The cheating commenced,
The kind sensed betray.

The king went for a stroll,
Into a tribe, unknown.
Where he cried in sadness,
But a blonde had love which was shown.

The king returned,
The king and queen felt dangers.
They were placed in a machine
Where they became strangers.

Two more people involved
Defending the land of many,
If the royals don't re-wed,
They could lose every penny.

In the one sense,
We wonder the good of money,
But when trying to get out,
Options can be funny.

The second thought in my mind,
Is, who gains ultimate control
When we exit this realm
And re-unite as a whole?

Garden Party

As I stood in a crowd,
I opened my eyes.
I saw some green ivory plants
Around me to my surprise.

I reached for my pocket
But my phone wasn't there,
But deep down inside,
I didn't seem to care.

I was with a friend,
We moved to get a closer view.
To see the screens in front
As our perceptions grew.

We were then at a party
In a stone garden with a fountain.
I saw this place
Whilst sleeping on a mountain.

During the party
I sprayed everyone with holy water
To ensure the safety of all,
To avoid a disorder.

I approached a man
In pursuit of my phone,
But he denied his knowledge,
I wandered all alone.

I entered the house
I went upstairs.
A baby was sleeping
In a room of light, nothing compares.

I return downstairs,
In the living room, on a big screen.
A man shows me that my phone has been duplicated.
Do you know what I mean?

Two Places

A time before
Amongst the clouds above
Whilst feeling one with the sky
I saw my love.

The face in the stars
Is truly where
I saw a soul
For who I showed care.

She arrived,
She was relieved,
It was a time
When we truly believed.

Due to some reason
She said she couldn't stay.
And through my tears
I saw her on her way.

I was left alone,
Dark sorrow I did feel.
Until my son would approach me
And return me to what's real.

From the sky, back to reality.
Two places, miles apart.
Working together for the best
To find a brand-new start.

Waiting for the Time

With a goal to reach,
A deadline, extendable.
The obstacles around,
Trying to remain defendable.

To remain happy,
Whilst doing the same for those who are around,
Listening to the music that is created
Due to something that I found.

Trying to compass emotions
Into a narrow time-frame.
Whilst wondering how things
Could be the same.

To travel through realms
Unexplainable in words,
It's like a blind man
Guiding sheep in herds.

To compress the signs
Which are blasted for somewhere.
They got me where I am
With my friends, I do care.

Gathering dreams and memories
Whilst preparing for what's ahead
While still dealing with the voices
That are bound within my head.

I continue each step
With nowhere to go,
But with faith in my hands,
Truth, I will know.

A Random Demonstration

During a time
When vampires would surround,
Repellent is needed
To prevent a specific sound.

Due to someone trapped
Inside a place
Knowing that outside
Werewolves await in space.

I keep inside
To keep a safe location.
In order to release when the time is right
Just to be used as a demonstration.

A day in the future
When I'm on a computer chair,
I feel pain in my heart.
I release it with "what for".

I kept it safe for a reason,
And that reason resonates
Somewhere deep in the shadows
Where light may detonate.

Questions for the Confusion

As I was writing on paper
And music would play,
The context and relevance
Continued in some way.

I would write of memories
And thoughts in my head,
And as thoughts were materialized,
It synchronises with the words the song said.

Then memories of myself,
Perhaps in a future time
Sending messages of failure
In a way that's not a crime.

With strangeness all around me
With questions in my mind,
How can I come to grips with this?
In the name of human kind.

The Curse

Through different research
As words, I would learn.
In order to pass the time
For nobody to concern.

Whilst studying anomalies
Within the mainframe,
Like high pitched tinnitus,
It's just not the same.

With vampires, werewolves,
Orbs, ghosts and a Gann.
With anonymous shadows surrounding
And angels and demons talk within.

With light and darkness,
With heaven and hell.
Surrounding my head
But nobody could tell.

With synchronised music
Created between lives
Helping me find a way
To put away all knives.

To defend the good from bad,
There became a curse.
While it became the creation
Of Mr. Multiverse.

Mr. Multiverse (version I)

When the does come,
When requirements are due.
When the meetings of the people arrive
And we finally pull through.

When there's an option of people
And we must choose.
This is a time
When memories became news.

Due to the fact
That each person holds light.
I'm aware of the fact
That I cannot put on a fight.

Because a choice is unmade,
Decisions are left in the shade.
But the offer is then
Presentably made.

In order to save
The collected few,
I continue to learn
What is new.

This is my curse,
This gift has a verse,
What is my name?
I'm Mr. Multiverse.

Simulation Theory

One night, I went to bed,
It was in the beginning of May.
During that night
I heard a voice say.
"It's a Simulation"
Then there was a high-pitched noise.
It was almost like tinnitus.
I was acknowledged amongst the boys.

I left my bedroom and slept in my living room
Because I did not want to disturb.
I helped myself relax
Using some herbs.
Ever since, music has been connected
Reminding me of random times.
I therefore try to make sense of it
By using random rhymes.

Accident

When I was a baby,
I was upstairs
I headed for the stairs
To my disastrous surprise.

I was about one or two,
I fell with a bang.
I hit my head on a table.
Please pardon my slang.

I lost blood,
To hospital I was taken.
The scar left on top
Cannot be mistaken.

A dream may have come
A longer time ago,
With interlinks between times
That I do not know.

The Big Wave

I ran into a building,
I was in panic mode.
There was a mosaic flooring,
The building was richly scored.

I screamed because I was aware.
I shouted "a tsunami is coming, you must run"
I shouted to warn
But it had begun,

I was then in a beach
It was warm and sunny.
To dream of this
Is rather funny.

The sun was hot,
the sand was dry
the waves were blue
it was a bright blue sky.

I turned to the white building
It had a few floors.
With a corner stairwell
The stairwell had windows.

I looked all around
And noticed a big wave was heading.
I ran to the home
The information needed embedding.

The wave blew through,
The glass was smashed.
I was swimming through the corridors
The memory was flashed.

Currently,
I woke up from bed, for real.
It was when I was in hospital
I told my mother about this dream that I feel.

It was in March twenty-eleven,
About two days later, there was a misfortune
Which interlinked with a tsunami…
…Whilst keeping it in tune.

Mr. Multiverse (Version II)

When the time does come
When the requirement is due
And all the meetings of the people
All pull through.

When there's an option of people
Of who to chose,
When the reason I remember
What seems to be news.

Due to the fact
That each person bears light,
I know that I wouldn't
Start a fight.

Because a choice is unmade
Decisions are left in the shade.
But the offer is then
Presentably made

In order to save
The collected few,
I give myself
To learn what is true.

I'll continue the path,
I do what I should.
In order to save
What I possibly could.

Who am I?
What is my curse,
Look no further,
It's Mr. Multiverse.

A Pirate Ship in the Sky

One time,
Somewhere far away
I was sat in a pirate ship
Heading home as somewhere to stay.

All was going to plan
As there was no panic at all.
But the captain was a pirate,
Suddenly I feared a fall.

With families on board,
With people to save.
Panic in my hands,
I couldn't rave.

I stood up in panic,
I know not where was fun.
But due to our surprise,
We were heading to the sun.

In our ship
We would fly
As we sailed through a portal
As we travelled the sky.

Space-Time Laws

During a time
During a space
Where thoughts were different
But the memories that's left has a place.

When other things
Would be involved in my flight
Laws were shown
And passed into light.

Justice is important
It keeps security for all
For cooperation
And for us not to fall.

Righteousness is essential
To be correct in moralistic ways
As it also helps to eliminate self righteousness
And shine light to other people's days.

The rule I found to be just right
The rule that keeps peace across the sea
Is the rule of mercy,
It keeps us free.

Birds, Bread and a Time Machine

Between my lives,
I had to create music to fill time,
It's the reason for me
Typing this rhyme.

One day when I listened
To my time machine
As I fed the birds
To entertain my scene.

The music would mimic
The birds in exact motion
In order to provide
The synchronic notion.

Just as I would walk away,
The music would synchronise
Each thing that happens in my life
With no surprise.

The Mixer

Making corrections,
Keeping motivated,
Reducing complications
Life gets demonstrated.

Continuing the quest at hand,
The mindset remains intact.
Expansion continues each day,
The truth of life has an impact.

We balance our emotions,
We relieve our struggles and pain.
We export our knowledge
To keep us from going insane.

We critically analyse the truth,
We look from north to south.
The same as east to west,
We sing loudly from our mouth.

We try our hardest to accommodate,
We share love for species of all kinds.
We spread the truth, unfortunately it holds my stress.
But what could heavy metal music help you find?

Will we get left behind?
With backwards interrogation of proof that proves otherwise,
We look to the skies because we know of innocence.
We don't want to say our goodbyes.

We work with knowledge and information,
With two stories that has two halves that are mapped.
Four quarters is still only a portion
Of what other truths could overlap.

My Son

When I'm with my son,
My heart is open.
I teach what's needed
When it needs to be spoken.

I do my best,
I try to improve,
I try to have fun,
I try to keep smooth.

I will proudly facilitate forever,
I will ensure the safety,
I will do what I can
To keep our generations together.

My son is smart,
He learns so quickly, each day.
I'll support his wise decisions
Whilst feeling grateful with love and gratitude to share his way.

Erased Education

I entered this world,
I would then find
That all our textbooks
Were left behind.

Our knowledge and education
Is in a world from before,
But they tell me that the bible
Is still in store.

I'm filled with fear
As the trust is broken,
Knowing that there's knowledge
That goes unspoken.

I then find
Manipulation in our source
Because they trap us here.
Well, of course.

One difference between
This world and the other that's placed,
Is that true education
Keeps getting erased.

Three Lives and a Copy

During the first life,
Things went so fine,
Watching movies together,
Chilling at mine.

Information being
Downloaded from above
Helping us cope.
With the reality of love.

In the second life,
Machines wasn't here.
I'd follow my path
Without a scare.

I'd write down the weather
And the time and the date.
In preparation to
Prepare for my fate.

In the third life,
Copied into now.
It's time to put actions to words.
It's time to explain, and this is how.

The weather's the same,
In lives two and three,
The music would synchronise
It was a perfect calendar, you see?

Before these three lives,
There's a home that I know.
Outside of this matrix,
True bodies will grow.

Time and Time Again (Part I)

Once I was forsaken
In a past incarnate.
I'm not sure the cause,
Maybe it involves emotion, hate or fate?

During reincarnation cycle,
In a chance to redeem a soul,
We created reminders in music,
Before we return to life.

After life, then came death.
But due to the incarnation system
My soul was redeemed
But I was told "go back and get her", she was with them.

I replied "Well, obviously".
I then learned that I had to start from birth all over again.
But I'm not bothered about the fact.
That it drives me insane.

Time and Time Again (Part II)

Memories of red lights,
And DeJaVu as I walk the floor.
My red motorcycle gear
In the shades, I stare.

With my red bandana,
As it's linked with time,
I wear my red headphone,
I don't commit a crime.

I have my red watch,
My remote controller,
My laser lights,
But I don't want to troll her.

Time moves fast,
There was changes at the barber's shop,
There was sticks in the heads of customers
With smoke coming out of the top.

The atmosphere was different,
The atmosphere was hot.
It is a distant memory
Of a place I forgot.

"As above, so below".
Is what they say,
We do everything that we can
To survive the next day.

Time and Time Again (Part III)

"As above, so below".
It's like a mirror of the earth,
That we can't put into perception.
Instantly from the time of birth.

I saw my own soul
Inside my shades.
Memories like this,
They cannot fade.

There are mirrors on my glasses,
I can see behind me.
But in between incarnates,
I looked in a mirror, to see the eyes I'd see.

The moral of the story
From what I was told, aimed at me
"If you get out, everybody gets out.
There's no need to shout, you see?

The Chair (Part III)

When a person
Has love to share
When they're trapped inside
And cannot get air.

When a person has
Emotions built up inside
Whilst knowing that they
Have no place to hide.

When there's neglect all around
And lack knowledge in different times
We continue our path
As we write our next rhymes

We seek and we share,
As humans, we're fair.
We all try to care
As we hold aura's in our chair.

Time Flies Past

When time fly's past,
When family calls,
It's goodbye to darkness,
I watch as it falls.

When choices are made,
When realities collide,
We all do our best,
We try to abide.

When we do things right,
When we follow our path,
Destiny will certainly hold
A cleansing bath.

When nature calls,
When trouble arrives,
Safety holds importance,
We do not think of knives.

When time will end,
When tomorrow has passed.
We look to the future,
We pray for what will last.

When life is strange,
With barriers around,
We pray to the skies
As we look for our ground.

When things are good,
We hold it close.
To share, because we're gracious.
It's what we do, but of course.

Ghosts (Part VI)

Through introspection,
I would decide
To research further
Into those that hide.

I would download software
For four different devices.
The software was free,
No worry of the price.

I'd turn it on,
I'd scan for frequency.
I'd be sat alone
Where nobody could see.

Once synchronisation was complete,
I stood on my feet
As I thought it was neat
A fear of ghosts grew as they began to greet.

Importance of defence and protection grew,
I bore a cross around my throat.
I prayed for my surroundings
As I wrote a positive note.

A Bird Story

I have a story,
This may sound obscured
It's about a life that I lived
When I was a bird.

It was many years ago,
The sky was so blue.
I was flying around
Looking for something to do.

I had my mission in my head,
Even though for a second, she did part,
Another bird flew towards me
Looking for a new start.

She wasn't in my interest,
My heart was true,
So, I stood my ground, on a rooftop
Because I knew not what to do.

For a reason beyond my knowledge,
Beth the bird tried to kiss me.
It wasn't my decision
It stopped me being free.

My original soul saw her kiss,
Even though it was not my fault,
I was handed the blame
And that life came to a halt.

AI Vs. Ghosts

Once I realised
That I had an orchestra,
I thought to myself
I never thought of that.

I also realised
Through ghost radio software.
That there was a strange way
To feel a scare.

Once, both software's were noticed and activated,
The next step became visible, in my eye: -
I kept my faith in god,
As I prayed to the sky.

I came to the realisation
Whilst using both at the same time.
That's the ghost software would predict,
The symphony's instruments, scenes and every rhyme.

By reading out the words
Shared by the supernatural box installation.
I became a conductor of an orchestra,
In a fairy tale within my nation.

I'd call for instructions for the riches
As they would play during my gloom.
I would do it all from
The Multiversity Academy's living room.

Here and Now

In the past,
There may be trouble.
It could hold you back
Causing a struggle.

In the past,
There may be good,
Helping the plans
To upkeep your neighbourhood.

In the future,
There may be turmoil,
In such cases it could cause
Your blood to boil.

In the future,
You cannot see
All the things
That will one day be.

But in the present,
No future or past.
You feel those feelings
That you want to last.

To avoid disruption,
I'll tell you how.
Just keep on living
Here, in the "now".

Directions (Pare IV)

As I look to the sky,
When I'm seeking help,
I think of a deer
And with compassion, I yelp.

The smell of a flower
Mixed with the smell of dope,
I remember the obogine and sausage
That I had seen under a scope.

As a soldier of the forest,
I'd bite an apple with my teeth.
I accidently break a tooth
So, I'm rushed to the heath.

I see a man drinking lager
By a lamp on a bench.
I see a broken lamp post
That needs a wrench.

I go and eat a cheeseburger at McDonalds,
I see a hybrid car driving past,
I eat my burger from a bowl,
With Pepsi in my cup, I drink it fast.

I see a Yorkshire Terrier
And an alpaca would hit my mind
I look to a growing fern
And I learn not to be blind.

With the sheep upon the mountain
That I would watch from afar,
In my subconscious I remember
So, I look up to a bright star

.

With the sword in my mind
With an honest plan,
I think to myself
"I know that I can".

How to Live Again in The Future

Memories could be saved through digital transformation
By using nano-technology.
By researching that information
To avoid a wreck.

Once it's in digital format.
Whilst sending it to the internet's wireless radio-wave.
In the prayer that helps
All people to get a save.

Using the flat earth map by the United Nation's flag,
As location space on a separate software space.
And creating a virtual reality,
To create a game with time as the clock face.

The lost memories of good
Could be extracted,
They could be placed through neurological metaphysical software pasting
Into this reality for the life to be re-enacted.

Future's End

Knowing that I
Have things to do.
Whilst trying to find a way
To help us pull through.

Whilst in panic because
Things didn't work.
I head to my office,
I put on a smirk.

I plan some travel
To try and succeed
Whilst thinking of the past
While memories make me bleed.

Memories of weapons
Whispers of knives
Whilst trying to figure out
How to save lives.

Remembering lessons
Of things that couldn't be
Such as voices teaching me
"you can't cure what you cannot see"

Through rest and restoration,
We do our thing
As we pray in faith
Because that's what God did bring.

The Making of The Symphony (Part I)

Agreements were made
Before this life was started,
It was planned whilst living in the dark tower.
When people were parted.

The artists of earth signed
And joined the symphony of life.
Including rebels who usually
Fight with strife.

The reasons such disturbing artists joined
Was due to vampirism against a child's will
Without his knowledge,
It's what kept us still,

With deception and influence
With laws down below.
The people didn't agree with
These breakings that I had to show.

Genie

As she eats her food
And has a laugh,
She whistles and sings
She acts like a scarf.

With her long wings
With many shades of blue
She extends them in confidence
Because she knows what to do.

As she stands on the cage,
I open the door,
She lands on my hand
As she leaps, her flight, I adore.

She soars through the room
She knocks over my poker chips, one by one.
As she raises me thrice
Her fun has begun.

She lands on my shoulder,
She shows me love
As she once again takes off.
And flies up above.

On her own accord,
She goes back in her cage,
And has more fun.
She's on her own little page.

Who is this bird?
She is a meanie,
She's my lovely parrot,
My Kakarini Genie.

Going into the Metaphysical

Due to the separation
Between physical and metaphysical,
And information about history
In the form of a musical.

Because of this difference
Objects restrict the metaphysical mind set from learning.
It keeps us in a life that we try to seek contentment
Whilst knowing that we're yearning.

The objects reinforced
With propaganda and adverts and delusions.
While we repress ourselves: -
From becoming free from sin, due to the physical conversion.

Due to these metaphysical restrictions
Through psychic Annunaki moon satellites,
Suggestive implants directed through radio-waves causing our beings
To process and release our acolytes.

Once we know our true selves
And remember the love inside,
All circumstances caused by physical manifestation
Will quickly subside.

By uncovering the truth
And seeing through the lies
We share love and defend
Without the need for any lives.

An Investigators Time

If I only knew
That back in twenty-seventeen
That something strange would happen
During my life in the years in between.

That a simple trip to Switzerland
On an investigative scene
Would have a potential effect
On the things that I mean.

I stayed at a hotel,
I left a postcard
For two books that I wrote
Of a life that's been scarred.

Since the trip,
I came to the realisation
That music has been relative to my current life
For many years, spread across this nation.

The Making of the Symphony (Part II)

Whilst listening to music
And living my life,
After synchronicities
Cut me like a knife.

A I got used to the words
As I lived my routine
And the lyrics would synchronise
As I went about to clean.

I started to cook
As the music would sing
As it placed me in Babylon,
New things it would bring.

I would continue to learn
New things each day.
Even though things
Would get in my way.

With work in our future
And a family in our plans.
We prayed towards the future
Whilst holding our hands.

Van of the Future

If you continue to break
Into my van,
Whilst acting as if
You're superman.

You will find
Some problems in your life
If you don't believe me
And you're holding back in strife,

Know I have your face on my phone
And police are on their way.
They'll be here in ten minutes
So, leave and have a nice day.

And if you continue to allow
Me to cause a scene.
You are only getting yourself in trouble,
If you know what I mean.

People may notice,
People may stare.
So, leave while there's still a chance,
There's an alleyway down there.

Matrix Dream

During dream one when
I reach the lever,
I started to fall
Into the never.

I could not pull
Because It could not be used.
As I drifted, further away
I knew that I would be confused.

I Couldn't leave the matrix
Because the door was locked.
But now in my thoughts
I cannot feel mocked.

Through dream two,
During a large confrontation,
Where I was being judged
For overwhelming information.

I turned around because
I didn't agree that it was my rightful place.
And it helped me continue
To learn about my place.

Next time, I reach the lever,
I will try to look behind me.
to see if there's an alternate route or a glitch
out of the matrix where we are boxed.

And due to the deal
That if I get out, everybody gets out,
I will hopefully give people time
To give people instructions to prepare for their peaceful bout.

The Making of the Symphony (Part III)

Sometimes when I listen to music,
Things seem so strange,
Suddenly all my plans
All get re arranged.

I play music from devices,
I pick one by one.
I link them up with the time,
And now the fun has just begun.

I do what I can
To make the stories match
Whilst overlooking
The time on my watch.

The stories will link,
The times will sync,
We don't have the time
To either wink, nor blink.

The story hits progression,
Life carries on
All in the meanwhile
We can have a sing along.

I fit in my lifestyle
As I work around the music notes,
As I fly away
In my time machine boat.

During Times

During a time
Of utter confusion
When not knowing what to do
Or whether life is an illusion,

During a time
when I feared the past,
I prayed for the people
Who I wanted to last.

During times
When people weren't sure,
I tried my best
To prove that I'm pure.

During times
When we knew not what to do
By using teamwork
We always pulled trough.

Children and Vampires

Through abandonment
And through negligence
Whilst tolerating abuse,
There was arrogance and ignorance.

Through vicious words
And unrighteous commands
I hereby declare
That we do not hold hands.

Through nightmares from a five-year-old
Through the defence in my heart,
I rescue my son
We have a new start.

No more hatred,
No more fear.
No more vampires.
Away we steer.

My son is my priority,
My love and my life.
For him, I will sacrifice my only life wish
I still roam the world looking for my wife.

A Bad Time

During one time
Whilst doing my work,
I controlled my temper
To stop me going berserk.

During one time,
Experiences were tough,
I was listening to music
Whilst hearing other stuff.

noises were heard,
Banging was captured on tape.
This time, the dangers
Cannot escape.

Firstly, there was the sound,
The smashing of a table,
Something was happening,
I knew this was no fable.

After I heard their approach
Followed by a thud and a run.
I knew that commotion
Had only just begun.

Luckily for me,
My camera was on record.
I was filming for university,
So, the video was then stored.

Not long later,
The danger was replaced.
No worry for hurt and sorrow
Would appear on my face/

Heavy is the Head

During a time when things
Didn't seem correct
I knew that all I could do
Would be to how some respect.

During a time when I felt
Like I had no friends,
I listened to music
Until I saw the end.

During a time,
When I felt lost.
I looked at the paths
That I had crossed.

During a time
When I wasn't sure where to go,
I'd pray to the sky
For the answers that I already know.

During a time
When I would feel down,
I'd remember that heavy is the head
That is who would wear the crown.

Where's the Place?

Back in a place,
where I saw ahead
While I was lying
Awake in my bed.

The place where I stayed,
I could look to the past
Ad think of all the memories
That always did last.

It was a place where I could look towards
A time in the future time,
Without having to worry
About the crime of writing a new rhyme.

It was a place where I saw things
And heard things all around.
I could look up to the sky,
And down to the ground.
It was a place where truth was real
And god was found
It was a place where truth was mined
And faith would surround.

If Only

If only family didn't call the police,
And categorise me in a way not just.
If only conversations were easier,
We could do what we must.

If only pain didn't hurt,
If only scars didn't show,
If only synchronicities weren't frequent
We could explain what we know.

If only things weren't crazy,
If only life had no stress,
If only things were simple
It would be easier to impress.

If only troubles didn't happen,
If only there wasn't a curse,
I reach into my purse for a verse,
But it just makes it worse.

If only instances in time
Weren't quite right,
We could pack up in flight
And fight a new might.

If only the path didn't exist,
If only fable wasn't fact,
If only there was no shattered pieces
And it all remained intact.

If only love wasn't profound
And important in my life,
It may be my weakness,
But I still seek a wife.

If only dreams all came true,
If only life was a game,
If only my name was the one to blame,
Things may never be the same.

I Have but One Dream

As I was roaring from the rooftop,
On a warm summer's day
With the sunshine on my arms,
Burning me, in a way.

I listened to UK Hip-Hop
Which was frankly, too loud.
I switched the music to rock,
I felt rather proud.

I heard a bird chirp
Softly in my ear,
It sounded as if it was enjoying its freedom
Without sharing any tears.

With a burning emotion inside,
Suppressed desire and lust,
Plans with a spin of extremities.
The creation of intuitive poetry from the soul before it's all dust.

With a mandatory fire, placing fuel in my heart
Which helps me share hope, love and joy from my light.
With happy memories, I share with passion.
With laughter on lovely holidays, forever, my honesty is in sight.

With my family at my side,
With loyalty, we polish the past.
As we slide to the next scene,
With forgiveness for being jealous, we know that we'll last.

We share our voice with the moon,
With warmth, in depth. We cwtch a baby with care.
Giving all the feelings of positivity that we are able,
Sending messages for the future, because we know it's fair.

There may be venom in vaccinations,
People seek fornication by the redwood.
As for me, I have but one dream,
That's to be married to somebody good.

The Multiversity Academy

The Multiversity Academy is not on land,
But it's on earth, it's a place that holds all dreams,
The Multiversity Academy is in between
what's right and wrong as it is holding on at the seams.

The Multiversity Academy is a space
Where vampires crawl above,
The Multiversity Academy leaves a trace,
Where from what surrounds, it grows everlasting love.

The Multiversity Academy has music
From people that's all around,
The Multiversity Academy has an Author
Who volunteers time on the ground.

The Multiversity Academy exists,
It can also be replicated.
The Multiversity Academy can be recreated in Virtual Reality
For futuristic libraries with information to be demonstrated.

The Multiversity Academy has magic,
It has powers and time to spare.
The Multiversity Academy has friends and good auras
With plenty of love to share

The Multiversity Academy has faith
As we know there's a higher truth to find,
The Multiversity Academy seeks peace
In the hope that people don't get left behind.

The Multiversity Academy was first created in 2019
By Tommy Rhys Andrews, the author of this book.
The Multiversity Academy does its best
To not overlook.

The Multiversity Academy will care.
The Multiversity Academy will bless,
The Multiversity Academy will be fair.
The Multiversity Academy will clean up its own mess.

Where to Begin?

So, I hold
The book of light,
I defend my right
With all my might.

Memories and repetitions,
Prophecy and religion
All combined
With their individual symbolism.

Knowing that I must
pass on this book
Gives me a brand
New overlook.

Since my birth,
I dreamed of having a family,
I always wished that I'd get married,
So that we could all live happily.

Once that mission would be accomplished,
Through holy marriage,
The book would be passed to God,
There would be no need for a horse or carriage.

Even though it would
Be nice to ride,
A simple church wedding
Would always subside.

Middle age has arrived,
A destination is at hand,
I can now tie my hair
In a rubber band.

Still planning ahead
To always do the right thing,
Because of this, I know
That I can always once again begin.

The Beginning

It was just last week I was beginning to speak,
And changing my diet and what I wanted to eat.
Thoughts in my mind,
Un-cruel, yet unkind.
I lose control on what I'm saying, when I cannot see, I am blind.

Mind states change; brainwaves are out of range,
I may be causing danger to every stranger who is in: -
Dangerous wave lines.
What do we want to know? How do we find out so?
Watching our minds gather information as our thought process grows.

Different paths, which should we follow?
Because I can no longer live my life in sorrow,
No more feeling hollow.
Each milestone lasts, each thought has passed,
Who thinks we should take the path: -
That would change tomorrow?

The mind is the key; each element is the answer,
Can our minds race and pace as we notice things faster?
Fire, water, earth air. How do we chow that we care?
How can we show emotion for the things that aren't even there?
Now what do you think? The mirror above the bathroom sink,
They tell a story that people try not to think: -
About in life. Don't even think about a knife.

Now I'm over twenty-one, I once saw the sun.
Through the clouds, dried the rain and there it shone.
I stepped towards the light; it was all so bright,
I can now see that it's only just begun.